To my children Arturo & Carla
—I don't know yet what they will become
But hey will manage quite a few projects, I'm sure

In 1989, Stephen Covey published his bestselling book "The 7 Habits of Highly Effective People" which was chosen the most influential business book of the 20th century, selling over 18 million copies worldwide translated into 38 languages. Many people see in the 7 Habits paradigm the keys to manage daily life better, but also to achieve sustainable long term effectiveness. In their path to effectiveness, lots of people have used the 7 Habits Covey's model for more than two decades. The 7 Habits framework has been adapted to families, teenagers, schools and corporations, always exceeding all expectations.

If somebody needs effectiveness more than anyone, this is the Project Manager. Very few professions are more objective oriented than Project Management. Besides, it is not a rewarding profession, since if the project is a success there is generally no reward for the Project Manager, but if it is a failure, then it will be his or her fault alone. Project work falls out of our area of control: we are supposed to coordinate what others do. Good habits make success in Project Management. As effective people, Project Managers should follow the 7 Habits Covey's paradigm, and of course his whole advice to seek our voice and inspire others at work, principle-centered leadership, personal planning, etc. This is necessary but not sufficient. Would we need a "character ethic" for Project Managers?

This book develops a structured model of the personal skills needed in order to be an effective Project Manager. It will allow you to learn, teach and practice the 7 Habits Covey's model in your profession of Project Management.

Jose Barato is the Director of PMPeople, which is a company specializing in Training, Consulting and Project Management. He is a telecommunications engineer, at the Universidad Politécnica de Madrid, with more than 15 years of experience in Project Management and IT Consulting. He has been PMP® certified since 2003 and PMI-Agile Certified Practitioner since 2013. Currently he is vice president and foundational member of the association PM-IB (Project Management Islas Baleares) and Director at PMI Madrid Chapter. He is the author of the books El Director de Proyectos a examen has a large experience as a PMP® certification exam trainer.

Foreword

If you are starting to read this book then you are concerned about your professional development. Since I met the author five years ago we have worked together many times. His drive, passion, interest and achievements on this field make him a good Project Manager and communicator. He knows how to sell good project management solutions for the twenty first century organizations. When Jose asked me to prologue this book I quickly said yes because I strongly believe that the development of a good professional never ends: We must improve our professional career with courage and carefully.

Throughout many years in this profession, I am truly convinced that soft skills are the key to have successful projects, successful Project Managers and successful organizations in the end.

Nature and animals bring us clear examples and lessons on this. For instance, if we pay attention to ants, we can learn many things about self-discipline, leadership, clear goals, effort, enthusiasm, persistence and patience. We can say ants are good on goal setting, team working and persistence when they carry on food from one anthill to another, or when they get prepared to possible attacks from other animals. We could say ants manage several projects a year. They have clear role and responsibilities for each team member. Ants are always connected. They can avoid obstacles to get their goals, but they are flexible and persistent enough to achieve them. They adapt to circumstances, prioritize, work in teams, respond positively the risks and never give up.

I would dare to define Jose Barato a tireless "ant" of Project Management. He does his best, works, shares and learns how to improve every day to reach new anthills.

I hope the reader enjoy those many good practices included in this book. Do not read this book just once. Go back to it many times. Those habits explained here require practice and persistence. Each of these habits is necessary and feasible. After nearly 30 years of experience as a Project Management "ant" myself, I learned that soft skills have a specific weight on project success. I also learned that we never stop learning —only the moment we die. This book will make your job as Project Manager more profitable and effective, mainly when challenged at working with people.

Think yourself, as a Project Manager, on each of the good practices described on this book. Today can be a great day for you. Do not wait for tomorrow to be aware of who you are, what project management soft skills you have, and what others you need to improve day to day. Start today and never give up.

Thanks very much, Jose, for your contribution to the profession with this book. It has been a real pleasure to prologue it.

TODAY IS A GOOD DAY!

Alfonso Bucero, DEA, PMP, PMI Fellow
Managing Director and President
BUCERO PM Consulting

Table of Contents

1. Good Habits make Success in Project Management.................1

2. Project Manager: Not quite a Rewarding Profession.................11
   Take your "Technical cap" off put your "Manager cap" on.................*15*
   Learning Managing Projects is like Learning Driving a Car.................*17*
   Let's accept the Role, know how to play, and play good.................*18*

3. The Project Manager must be a "Good Person".................25
   A Regretful Personal Experience.................*29*
   Personality Ethic versus Character Ethic.................*32*
   Principle Centered Project Management.................*34*
   Old Paradigm Centered Project Management.................*39*
   The Project Manager's Essential Body Parts.................*51*
   A Character Ethic for Project Managers.................*53*

4. The 7 Habits of Effective Project Managers.................57
   Habit 1. Committing to the Project.................*63*
   Habit 2. Planning Progressively.................*77*
   Habit 3. Controlling the Project.................*93*
   Habit 4. Negotiating (Win-Win or No Deal).................*113*
   Habit 5. Communicating (Empathic Listening).................*137*
   Habit 6. Leadership (Team Growing).................*163*
   Habit 7. Performing Better the Next Project.................*189*

5. Maturing as an Effective Project Manager.................197
   Let's assume the Role, know how to play, and play good.................*201*
   Dependent Project Managers.................*204*
   Independent Project Managers.................*206*
   Interdependent Project Managers.................*209*

6. Appendix 211
  I. Performance Appraisal for Project Managers 213
  II. Code of Ethics and Professional Conduct by PMI® 221
  III. Denver International Airport (Case Study) 233

1

Good Habits make Success in Project Management

-The fastest path between two points is a straight line?
-No
- The fastest path between two points is the one of least resistance?
-No
- The fastest path between two points is the one you know better?
-No. The fastest path between two points is the most beautiful!

ALEJANDRO JODOROWSKY

1. Good Habits make Success in Project Management

In this era of the Knowledge Society, with most added value being produced by knowledge workers, we hear the word "project" when discussing new product developments, professional services, IT enhancements, engineering endeavors, organizational changes, business process improvements, etc. In each private company or public administration, top managers have to select the most appropriate investment options; medium managers have to perform overall supervision of the works required to deliver agreed investments and finally, Project Managers have to develop specific planning and control the implementation of each single approved initiative. Most efforts inside organizations are related to projects, and there is always a Project Manager to ask about project performance. On this context, Project Managers outstand among others knowledge workers, increasing day by day their level of responsibility and authority. Many Project Managers have a catalytic role within organizations. They are true leaders highly valued. They inspire others and make change possible. Could be Project Management the profession of the future?

In this professional environment more and more interdependent of Knowledge Society, we will still be having *blue collars* (developing the technical work), there will still be having *white collars* (taking care of strategy and finance) and filling the gap, we will have *Operation Managers* to run the business and *Project Managers* getting changes done effectively.

> *In the Knowledge Society, we will have Blue Collars, White Collars and filling the gap, getting things done effectively, we will have Operation Managers and Project Managers*

> *An Effective Project Manager is the one who consistently deliver on Time, on Cost, on Scope, meeting the Quality standards*

In order to be effective as Project Managers, we need to consistently deliver (project by project) on time, on cost, on scope and meeting the quality standards. Is there a professional career to become an Effective Project Manager? Should you get some kind of accreditation? Should you get proficient on project management tools? Should you improve your soft skills, sales skills, domain expertise?

As far as I know, those who succeed as Project Managers don't necessarily have any of the above attributes. The Effective Project Managers I know have one thing in common: They are people of good habits. They manage guided by principles.

I think it is necessary, but not sufficient, that they know about tools and techniques, good practices of management and industry, and apply lessons learned. But in order to get things done, and to get stakeholders satisfied, they have to have a character based on good habits.

> *The unique recipe to Project Success: Let's apply Good Habits (based on Principles)*

Any project is a kind of natural (not artificial) system, in the sense that you are not capable of controlling so many variables affecting the project. We can say projects resemble agricultural work: they follow *The Law of the Harvest*.

The farmer has to do the right thing the whole year, and in the end, *if he is lucky*, he will have a good harvest. In a project there are no shortcuts. Project Managers have to do the right thing during the whole project lifecycle. They have to apply good habits of committing, visualizing, executing, negotiating, communicating, leading, learning, etc. In the end, *if they are lucky*, the project will succeed. If a Project Manager has a character based on good habits, it is likely (not certain), that the project ends on time, on cost, on quality and with the required functionality. Apart from the product, other important and rarer result is a synergic cohesive team.

We Project Managers are mostly judged by results. This is not quite a rewarding profession: If we meet the goals, no one will praise us[1]. If we don't meet the goals everybody will criticize us. But the most of the project work falls out of our area of control: we are appointed not to do, but to manage what others do. Projects don't usually fail just because of technological issues. You can easily find the required technical expertise among team members quite often. A project may fail *just because team members John and Mike don't even talk to each other*. The absence of soft skills in project management is often the root cause of failed quality control and scope validation, low productivity of the team, high level of rework, slippages, cost overruns, etc. Our profession demands more of Sociology and less of Technology.

> *Projects need more Sociology and less Technology: A Project can fail just because John and Mike don't even talk to each other*

---

[1] More on this matter in chapter 2: Project Management is a goal oriented job.

You may have had some experience with a Project Manager you didn't like. If you have to work with an ineffective Project Manager, what do you think of him? What attributes of him upset you most? If you happen to be in a position to contribute to his performance appraisal, you may have ever written down some of the expressions below:

- *He is always complaining about the organizational processes, the lack of resources, the customer, the deadlines, etc., but he never proposes any solution.*

- *He is not a proactive person. He does not anticipate problems. He proceeds reactively, crisis after crisis.*

- *He takes too long to make any decision. I don't see him having clear criteria regarding the project.*

- *He has not prepared any formal or informal project plan. If I ask him, he does that, but I suspect it's just for the record.*

- *He does not manage time well. He is always overwhelmed. He never seems to have time for anything new. He does not respond to email. He does not call back. The urgent does not let him do the important. He is not used to keeping his promises.*

- *He is not used to delegating. He has to take every decision himself. He goes too deep on technical details.*

- *He is too authoritarian. He has burned the team out. I also have so many complaints from the functional managers, from the client, from the sellers, etc. He has not a good rapport with stakeholders: they don't trust him.*

- *He lacks the drive to close the project. He has the 90% complete syndrome.*

- *I see him making the same mistakes. He stumbles over the same stone twice. I think he is not concerned about improving.*

▪ *He does not maintain a project log. He does not manage scope well. He says the client yes to everything.*

▪ *He is not concerned about the budget, the actual costs, the invoiced cost, the financial margin, etc.*

▪ *He does not provide executive reporting. For instance, he is not able to measure the current progress, nor forecast the final slippage and cost overrun.*

Take notice that only the last three bullets are related to hard skills. Most of ineffective Project Managers are criticized for lacking soft skills. A project could fail simply because two team members are always fighting, or because the team has a low morale, or because we don't understand client requirements.

Effective Project Managers are role models to personal effectiveness, but they are even more outstanding in inter-personal effectiveness: they are used to getting public victories. They are real experts in negotiating, communicating, leading, and they never stop learning. They rarely become Effective Project Managers through quick fixes, tricks, manipulating or deceiving others. Overall, we think of them that they are "good persons". They have a good character, forged with good habits. They play a referential (not positional) leadership, based on principles: They are honest, responsible, respectful, integral, humble, trust worthy, persistent, patient, etc. They may not be very eloquent, but it is a pleasure to work with them and for them. They may not be subject matter experts in the field, but they always know the name of the expert to call.

When leading projects to success, there is no shortcut. To form and develop good Project Managers, it is not enough just to do it by tolling, training, standards or books. Credentials and complete training programs are not enough neither.

Many projects turn into vital experiences. Projects are rarely entirely determined since the beginning. Quite often, the project is a continuous process of discovery, re-planning and re-aligning. Every project is a collective experience of growth. After living a challenging project, producing a synergic team, people are not the same anymore. These projects mark our lives: there is a before and after.

When a project is a painful, unpleasant, regretful experience, one thing is certain: it will end late, with poor quality and cost overrun. Project Managers are judged by goal achievement, true, but in this profession the means counts as much as the end.

> *When managing Projects, the Means*
> *counts as much as the End*

To be an Efficient Project Manager, you enjoy uncertainty. You accept that projects are prone to problems. To get wise solutions, you involve the people in the problems and seek the solutions with them.

When working or leading a project, you better "live" that project as a complete person. Stephen Covey represented the complete person paradigm with a circle of four sections, one for each type of intelligence: the body (physical intelligence), the mind (mental intelligence), the heart (emotional intelligence) and the spirit (spiritual intelligence).

Let's see how to translate these four intelligences into Project Management.

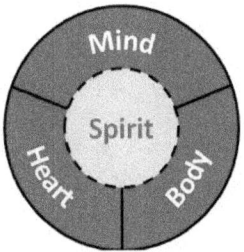

- **Body**: To follow a strict discipline to execute the plan. To align goals to results.
- **Mind**: To compose a complete mental image of the project and its parts. To continuously visualize results and the way to achieve them.
- **Heart**: To seed trust among team members. To get them know how to do and get them do that by themselves.
- **Spirit**: To feel the transcendent contribution of the project in the bigger scheme of things.

Each project needs a lucky strike, but luck usually comes if we are really connected. Apply a principle centered leadership to take the right decisions. Live your project being present and aware. To get public victories in your projects, don't take the fastest or easiest path: *take the most beautiful one.* The most beautiful path to lead a project is t*he one which let you and your team members grow as complete persons.*

> *When managing projects, the fastest and most beautiful path is the is the one which let us grow as complete persons*

1. Good Habits make Success in Project Management

2

Project Manager: Not quite a Rewarding Profession

Why can't I be good
Why can't I act like a man
Why can't I be good
And do what other men can
I'd like to look in the mirror
With a feeling of pride
Instead of seeing a reflection
Of failure a crime

LOU REED: Song "Why can't I be good"

2. Project Manager: Not quite a Rewarding Profession

After many years in the profession, I've met many people who claimed to be Project Managers, but actually they weren't. Even worse, they didn't have the attitude to become one. These people found their comfort zone (they didn't recognize that, though) in deciding and executing every single technical detail, so proficient in their domain of expertise that no one could do their job, catch up their pace, deal with crisis, handle complaints, etc. When leading project teams, they did not delegate many technical tasks, as they tried to control team members' work by controlling over the technical details, discussing on "how to do" more than on "what to do".

What they had in hand, was it a project? We can say yes: There were goals, requirements, testing, milestones, a team, a schedule, a budget, etc. There was also a project code to allocate time and expense sheets.

However, in my humble opinion, these people did not manage projects: They did not manage their work according to a plan, they changed scope every day (provided that they had defined one!), they did not anticipate potential problems, and they were not proactive nor predictable. Let's not call this project management, then. Let's use a more appropriate name instead: Let's say they managed operations, services, technical assistance, supporting, etc.

The reality check used to come when the big crisis exploded: The project was losing much money, it was seen as impossible to achieve goals, or what was delivered was "unacceptable, poor quality" according to the client, etc. Then the proposed solution used to be to replace that Project Manager with a new one. This caused harm for client, for the selling organization this Project Manager belonged to, not to mention the low morale of the dismissed Project Manager, who was totally identified with the project, for sure. If you are a Project Manager like him, if you *are* the project, if you take every criticism as personal, then when you are released as the Project Manager in charge, and another colleague takes over, how would you feel?

In projects there is much on stake. There are many stakeholders: people who win or lose because of the project. Chances are for project success, but chances also are for project big failure, sometimes impacting the company image or even the stock market's share value. There is no other profession in the world more goal oriented than project management. Project Management is definitely not quite a rewarding profession: If goals are met, as they have to be, that is the reason you are in charge, then no one praise you. But if goals are not met, then the fault is only yours. While everything was doing okay, nobody said a thing, but now that everything is going bad, suddenly, everyone is talking about risk management, poor documentation, poor leadership, quality audits, communication problems, lack of social skills, convenience of coaching, etc. The result is always the same for the poor Project Manager: Everybody blames us and we don't have good defense.

A distinctive point when comparing "technical success" to "Project Management success" is that the technical guys depend mostly on themselves, but the success of Project Managers depend much on external variables, most of them out of their control zone: team, client, sellers, resources, performing organization, luck...

If there are so many factors against us, if we are so badly judged, if we don't deserve a second chance (we are replaced!) Why would anyone want to become a Project Manager?

May everyone explain their own way: I love this profession because no other is more suitable for changing this world in we live.

Take the "Technical cap" off. Put the "Management cap" on

When performing post-mortem analysis on a failed project, we usually see that projects rarely fail because of technical problems. Can you imagine a web portal project failing because an unacceptable response time? or doesn't work well for more than 100 concurrent users? or images are not well displayed in smart phones because of using flash technology? These are common technical issues easy to solve. Sometimes, technical issues are critical ones, though (imagine you lack an expert in a new technology, for instance), but in general, you can easily find the required technical expertise among team members quite often. The root causes of project failures have more to do with:

- Poor Risk <u>Management</u>
- Poor Cost <u>Management</u>
- Poor Stakeholder <u>Management</u> (client, team, sellers, etc.)

However, most Project Managers are just technically proficient: Since they have good domain expertise, they are supposed to lead teams and projects, so they are put in the position of a Project Manager —this is called "the halo effect". But technical knowledge is not enough to manage projects. Effective Project Managers don't do the work: they just make team members to do the work —like an orchestra director, they don't play the instruments. A Project Manager is the prime project responsible, but they have also the authority level to take decisions. She or he needs to focus on real management, not in detailed technical issues.

> *A Project Manager should remember "taking the Technical cap off and putting the Management cap on"*

Bad news: Putting the management cap on is not easy. Think of the best Project Manager you know. Yes: that one who consistently deliver on time, on cost, on scope, meeting quality standards, and properly managing expectations of stakeholders —customer, team, organization. That one who make bosses fight for, whose team every team member wants to belong to, that one who knows how to anticipate problems (he rarely press the "crisis" button"), to whom customers worship. Where do you think he learned everything? Not in books!

Like every complex discipline, Project Management is learned by practicing. This is a continuous learning process, each project a new challenge, true lessons mistakes made.

Good news is that there is some help —all a Project Manager may need is already invented:

- The body of knowledge applying every project is perfectly structured in the PMBOK® guide.
- You should never stop learning Project Management, but knowledge areas are limited: there are only 9, according PMBOK® version 4th.
- Each project is different, but there are 42 management processes applying them all, and a very recommendable set of tools, techniques and document templates.
- You don't have to reinvent document templates to declare the project approval, formulas to measure cost and schedule performance, etc.
- At least, there is a "common language" to manage projects, and we can say that it is a good thing that there are reusable processes, templates, suggested deliverables, frameworks, methods, organizational processes assets, etc...

> *All a Project Manager may need is already invented*

Learning Managing Projects is like Learning Driving a Car

You don't become an Effective Project Manager overnight. You need practicing. In a way, *learning managing projects is like learning driving a car*:

- You can drive without a license, only inside a private property and short travels. In the same way, you can get experience in Project Management with short low risk projects.

- To get your driving license you have to study the driver license manual and to pass an exam of two parts: theory and practice. The equivalence in Project Management is to study the PMBOK® and to take the PMP® exam (you don't need a practice exam but you need to credit enough experience having managed projects in the past).

- You don't leave driving school as an experienced driver. You learn by practicing (there are many lifelong poor drivers!). Getting your PMP® doesn't mean you are a good Project Manager. To maintain the credential you need to keep updated but more important: you keep on managing projects.

- When driving, you respect traffic rules. When managing projects, you abide PMI's Code of Ethics and Professional Conduct. You also follow the organizational process standards and regulations applicable to the performing organization.

- When you drive, you don't carry your driver manual in the dashboard. When you take driving decisions you don't need to read the book. You rely on your knowledge. You drive, you decide, you are accountable. It is important to drive well, but it is more important to get to your destination. In a similar way, you lead your project to achieve the goals. Knowledge is in your mind, not in manuals.

Accept the Role, know how to play, and play good

There is no other more goal oriented profession in the world than Project Management. This is not quite a rewarding profession, though: If goals are met, then no one praises you. If they are not, then it's entirely your fault. If we agree on this, then we should recognize that Project Management has much to do with attitude.

> *Project Management has much to do with attitude*

An Effective Project Manager has to assume his or her role, know how to play the game, and play good. If a beginner Project Manager were to ask about the rules of the game of Project Management, how could that be?

Let's see a fictional dialogue below. When I was a beginner, these would have been the questions I would have asked and the answers I would have expected, more or less:

Game rule #1: Commit Yourself

–They put me in charge of a critical project. They have appointed the team members. They have set the goals, the budget, the schedule; but they have also made me accountable of the whole thing. Is this good or bad?

–Congratulations! This is something good for you. This means the company you are working trusts you. You have a challenge ahead, much to learn and to demonstrate.

Game rule #2: Deal with Constraints

–It seems like I'm stumbling brick walls again and again. What do I do?

–As professor Randy Paush[2] said: "Brick walls are there for a reason. The brick walls are not there to keep us out; the brick walls are there to give us a chance to show how badly we want something. The brick walls are there to stop the people who don't want it badly enough. They are there to stop the other people!"

Game rule #3: The Ends justify the Means many times

–Most things lay beyond my control zone. What should I do?

–Most projects are not very predictive. They are prone to problems and uncertainties. If that is the case, not having clear authority boundaries is normal. Many times, as a Project Manager, you have to question about limits. For the benefit of the project, in order to get things done right, stakeholders will tolerate if Project Manager skips some authority levels, or does not do everything by the book. In this profession, the ends justify the means many times. On this subject I recall the inspirational text A Message to Garcia[3]. The expression "To Carry a Message to Garcia" is often used when getting things done in an environment of uncertainty, acting beyond one's circle of influence.

---

[2] Randy Pausch was a professor at the Carnegie Mellon University. He got worldwide recognition after his lecture for 400 students on September the 18th of 2007, on how to achieve the childhood dreams. He was ill with cancer: http://goo.gl/BgUoK

[3] You can read the original text at: http://goo.gl/I9S2g

Game rule #4: Always keep an Updated Credible Plan

–I've just analyzed what the client has been promised, and to be honest, I think it is impossible to meet the goals. I know I'm supposed to be planning right now, but I don't see the point in doing so.

–Everyone may think you are not a good professional if you don't have a plan, so you better have one which is realistic and credible to stakeholders. Take the time to elaborate a feasible plan. Propose sensible alternatives. This problem is not only yours: involve the stakeholders and seek the solution with them.

Game rule #5: When you don't know, take Assumptions

–There are many things of this project that I don't know yet. It seems impossible to me to estimate durations, costs, resources, etc. What should I do?

–You can perform progressive planning elaboration. For the purpose of estimating, you can take assumptions. You can say, for instance: *Assuming this seller will deliver the hardware on time, assuming team members have this productivity rate, assuming the client assign the key resources I need to validate requirements when they are due, assuming... then I can estimate our deadline between April the 20th and May the 15th, with a confidence level of 65%.* You will check continuously if assumptions are still valid. You will keep an updated planning as you discover new information about the project.

Game rule #6: Manage the Project by Managing its Risks

–This project is prone to uncertainty. I keep talking on risks all the time, but everybody seems to ignore them. What should I do not to be blamed when problems materialize?

–*Words are gone with the wind.* You better keep an updated risk register. Risk management is the opposite of crisis management. It is the only way to anticipate problems. As a Project Manager, you want to have problems; you don't want to be shocked. When problems materialize, you will give a professional image if you anticipated them and you had a planned response. On each follow-up meeting, you assign time to risk management (it may be enough if you review only the most important ones). When you describe a risk, don't forget to communicate the risk exposure expressed in money terms. If response is to accept, then take note of when and who decided in your risk register.

Game rule #7: Adapt Communication to Stakeholders

–My boss' boss wants to be noticed of everything, but he doesn't come to any follow-up meeting. One day the client is going to call him to complain, he is not going to know what to respond, and it will be a cascade of reprimands until me. How should I avoid this?

–It is perfectly normal that high executives don't have the time to assist project meetings, but this is not the only way to let them know. Communication has to be adapted to stakeholder. In these cases it is very useful to produce a periodic status summarized report; dashboards with color health check indicators; milestone schedules, etc.

Game rule #8: Practice Incremental Iterations to Mitigate Risks

–It seems to me this client does not know what he wants. What he is demanding is too loose and ambiguous. When we deliver the product, he is going to say "No" to everything. What should I do?

–You should practice incremental iterations. You deliver once part of the product each time, first the important ones. This way they can validate progressively. Clients generally don't know what they want, but they always know what they don't want. You may have your fist delivery 100% rejected, you will do rework and defect repairing. You likely have the second delivery not totally rejected (and you validate completely the first one). This incremental validation dynamic will allow the client to model his vision of the final product progressively. This is just common sense risk management: If you get the client to say 20 times "Yes, but..." then finally he is going to say "No".

Game rule #9: Fight Scope Creep!

–The client wants to introduce changes continuously.

–You won't allow that. If scope is changing every day, then you simply are not managing any project. Scope creep is the worst enemy for a Project Manager. An effective technique to avoid scope creep (among others) is an integrated change management system.

Game rule #10: Trust your Team

–The assigned team members do not have much previous experience in something like this project. They have never worked together. It seems that the only real expert is me. I cannot replace anyone on this group. Should I have to do most of the work myself?

–Of course not. If team members need training, you have to get them take the training. On the other hand, you can practice a situational leadership, adapting your leadership style to the maturity of your team. You first will have to direct them tightly, then you assign roles and have them understand why they do things (*you let them make mistakes*). After a while, they will need you only some times, and beyond a date, they will be self-sufficient. A synergic team will be good for you, but it will be better for your organization: they will be a true invaluable company asset.

If you are an Effective Project Manager, you are an important company asset as well. Today's companies demands people like you because there are more and more projects in their portfolios, and they are more and more critical and complex. In many companies, projects are the only things you can see around.

> *In many companies, Projects are the only things you can see around*

2. Project Manager: Not quite a Rewarding Profession

3

The Project Manager must be a "Good Person"

Sow a thought, and you reap an act
Sow an act, and you reap a habit
Sow a habit, and you reap a character
Sow a character, and you reap a destiny

ANONYMOUS

3. Project Manager must be a "Good Person"

There was a time when I thought every problem in life could be fixed using the proper tool or technique. We human beings won the evolution race thanks to our ability to use tools, didn't we?

Just being proficient in enough tools you could succeed in live:

- Do you want to be good at judo? You learn the techniques; train your best throws, locks, joints and strangulations. In competition, you better be left hander, avoid the grip; rub the opponent face with your kimono. You can catch your breath by loosening your belt: the referee will give you some seconds to get you dressed properly.

- Do you want to be a good student? Get good lecture notes and past exams samples. Study hard the days before the exam. Put your best effort in the subjects more likely to be asked. Get a good lab partner.

- Do you want to learn English? Enroll yourself in an immersion course. Take face-to-face classes from a native teacher. Get your children cared by an American or English *au pair*. Go abroad on holidays.

- Do you want to be a good software programmer? Don't worry about software quality: you better be the only one to understand your code. Your job is finished if compilation is passed. Testing is none of your business. Don't worry about integration: you just make your code interface compliant. Use as much external code libraries as you can, this way you can finish earlier, and failures are not your fault. Exaggerate the technical impact of any change. Get functional problems out of your responsibility.

Now I have two kids. I don't want them to study the last minute, just for the exam. I want them to master the subjects and develop an educated mind. I want them to work hard every day: to be more "ant" than "grasshopper". I don't want them to manipulate others. I want them to be trustworthy. I don't mind if they are not very eloquent, I prefer them to be honest. Something tells me that they will succeed in life if they forge a habit based on principles.

When I was preparing my PMP® exam, I thought it was weird to prepare about responsibility, fairness, respect and honesty. When I was told that a Project Manager has to be a "good person" it seemed to me like one of those self-help books. Good values may help if you manage large projects in the USA, or if you work for the NASA, for instance. To be responsible, fair, respectful and honest may be helpful for very big projects, or projects at high risk. In my organization environment, for the software projects I managed, I usually had to skip about the ethics, didn't I?

> *To be successful in our projects, do we have to skip about the Ethics?*

I used to think so, but I don't think like this for a long time.

A Regretful Personal Experience

Some years ago, the company I worked for won a very promising contract. The project consisted of developing a technological strategy plan for a Public Administration Organization. This project was considered "key" in an almost literal sense: we'd need it to be able to gain access to future projects.

High profile consultants needed were based in Madrid, but this project would be executed in the client offices in another city in Spain. Due to cost constrains, consultants would work remotely. Since this project was the most critical in this region, the Functional Manager was appointed as the Project Manager. I was leading one of the five subprojects in Madrid.

The project was closed seven months late (100% behind schedule), with a cost overrun as high as three times the original budget. Regarding personal relations, every consultant ended up burned out, not willing to deliver any high quality consulting product, nor keeping involved in future projects there, nor helping that Project Manager anyway (only if obliged).

So what happened? Here is a short list of the explanations from my side:

- The five different consulting teams in Madrid worked disconnected most of the time.
- The common feeling regarding the work process was like this: "I belong to a pool of experts. As in an assembly line, the text I produce will be inserted into a bigger document that I don't' need to know".
- The project lacked a clear scope and schedule. Team members hardly had a sense of the bigger picture. Maybe only at the end, if they did.

- In order to progress, we were always in reactive mode:
  - The client demanded something new;
  - the Project Manager translated his own directions to team leaders;
  - consultants produced the documents that...
  - ...that Project Manager felt free to change and integrate (he did not have time to get the consultants' approval)
  - ...and finally, he delivered the presentation to the client by himself.
- The Project Manager banned direct access to the client personnel. If the teams needed to validate some work in progress to the client, they previously had to get his approval.
- The Project Manager did not confront people conflicts. He preferred to deal with the team leaders, or with the team leaders' bosses. Escalating these problems just made them worse.
- Most of the stakeholders, from team members to middle and top managers, felt continuously manipulated and deceived by him.

In short, we all distrusted that Project Manager. The project in fact was a failure in all senses. But please notice the curious line: *This Project Manager suffered no pain.*

When you control the whole communication, you can always provide the best excuses:

- The client was not satisfied in the end: "Consultants from Madrid were not able to translate their theoretical models into the local idiosyncrasy."
- The project has been too behind schedule: "Besides managing operations in this region of Spain, I had to devote most of my time to this project, and I was the one to take all decisions. Accountable people in Madrid did not involve enough to be delegated."
- The Project had suffered much rework and consequently, much cost overrun: "The client couldn't approve documents as delivered. First versions were misaligned by far. I had to rework everything, but I was alone on this."
- No team member trust you, they don't want to work with you anymore: "I have had to be authoritarian many times. If not, the work simply was not made. As you can see, this has damaged my relations with my workmates. I hope management will know how to reward this personal sacrifice."

Wait a minute. How could that be possible? You remember from chapter 2 that Project Manager is the first to fall when project falls. Is this some kind of contradiction? I don't think so. In chapter 2 we discussed the common problems of a *regular practitioner* in project management. This was a *Functional Manager* leading the project. He did not do well as a Project Manager. *He only was not found out.*

I'm not aware if he has managed more projects afterwards. I hope this regretful experience directed him to a career more focused on sales, or business administration. I hope that today he has a position that entitles him to delegate on a Professional Project Manager whenever a critical project in his region has to be managed.

Personality Ethic vs. Character Ethic

Many business schools continue preparing business executives in the **Personality Ethic**. The effectiveness paradigm for these institutions goes like this: Effectiveness is a function of personality, of public image, of attitudes and behaviors, skills and techniques that lubricate the processes of human interaction. That is, people can be effective by applying techniques, adapting their conduct or attitude, manipulating others as if they were things. According to Covey, many people achieve this kind of "secondary greatness" (that is, social recognition for their talents) but they lack "primary greatness" (or goodness in their character).

On the other hand, the effectiveness paradigm based on the **Character Ethic** says we don't get effective by shortcuts or quick fixes, but by applying principles such as responsibility, respect, fairness and honesty[4]. Covey discovered there are universal principles that govern human effectiveness. If you don't follow those principles, you could be effective in the short term, but not in a sustainable way. Effectiveness relies on each person's character. A character of effectiveness (in both sides private and public) is built with 7 main habits, and those habits are based on principles.

Principles govern the consequences of our behavior. Principles are not esoteric, mysterious nor religious ideas. They are self-evident and may be validated. They are part of the human condition, of human conscience. Some principles are, to name a few: responsibility, respect, fairness, honesty, integrity, dignity, humbleness, loyalty, temperance, encouragement, excellence, contribution, patience, potential, growth, compassion, synergy, etc.

---

[4] These four principles are developed in Code of Ethics and professional Conduct by PMI®. This document can be downloaded at http://www.pmi.org

Principles are natural laws that can't be broken. The consequences of not following them are clear enough: As free human beings we could choose to jump out a window, but we cannot ignore the consequences of the gravity law. Principles are not values. Values tell us how things should be. Hitler had values, but he had no principles. There are good and bad values, and good values are based on principles. Covey said: "While values drive behaviors, principles govern consequences."

Any project is going to fail if the Project Manager is a liar, or if he wastes the money not wisely, or does not respect other team members, blames others for his own mistakes, seeks just his personal gain, takes credit for the merits of others, etc. He may get some punctual and quick success. Maybe nobody is aware of his bad manners this time. But one thing is for certain: He is not investing for future success as a Project Manager.

Project Managers with a track record of success are usually good in hard and soft skills, but more important for them is this: Leadership for them is a choice, not a position. Effective Project Managers have a Character Ethic: They apply a Principle Centered Leadership.

> *Effective Project Managers applies a*
> *Principle Centered Leadership*

Principle Centered Project Management

If you are about to hire a Project Manager, you may like to know if he is familiar with project management tools, his academic background, if he is a PMP® certified since when, how many projects has he managed, his industry expertise, etc. One candidate may score high at these topics, yet I would hesitate if hiring him or not.

Conversely, sometimes you don't need to ask anything. Someone else comes along, and a little voice inside you sings out, "It's her! She is the one! Grab her and put her in charge of the whole works and leave her alone". That's the gut speaking. Her résumé don't say much, but she starts talking... and you already know for sure. You want her to manage the project. It is a critical project, and if it goes wrong it is going to make a great loss for everybody, but in some way, you know you have made the right decision.

When I perform hiring interviews, my main concern is to get to know if this person will be effective because of having good habits. Here is a sample of main topics I usually ask (they are 7 main topics not by accident):

1. Is he used to committing? Is he used to identify goals? Is he proactive? Is he used to getting into the role of a Project Manager?
2. Is he used to clarifying what to do, early enough?
3. Is he used to controlling scope, schedule and cost? Is he used to doing the talk, to getting things done?
4. Is he used to managing uncertainty? Conflicts? How are his negotiating skills?
5. Is he used to communicating effectively?
6. Is he a good leader?
7. Is he used to continuous learning?

> *If you want to know if you are hiring an Effective Project Manager, check out his or her habits*

The answers to these questions offer plenty of good information, but in general, you get the best information not from what they answer, but what they ask, and also from what they don't ask:

- If he does not ask good questions, would he be good at communication, negotiation, leadership? Would he be able to get stakeholder's requirements?
- If he does not ask about his level of authority, his empowerment to take decisions, would he be truly committed to project goals?
- If he does not ask about his expected wage, bonus, increase rate, would he be a got negotiator? Would he know how to manage project costs?
- If he does not ask about enterprise environmental factors, quality standards, follow up procedures, would he be a good communicator?
- If he does not ask about his team, working conditions, most frequent issues regarding human resources, current capacity and skills, training plans, turnover rate, etc. Would he be a good leader?

Throughout any project lifecycle, the Project Manager has to take a lot of decisions, in a day to day basis. Overall, these will be the right decisions if the Project Manager is effective both in private and public sides. I'll try to explain this point with a real case from my experience.

One of the worst experience I had to live as a Project Manager had to do with two people that did not fit into a team. These two people were high experts on *mainframe*[5] technology. I had to integrate them into an already formed team of eight people: experts on the "new" Java technology, much younger, with a different style of working.

We worked at the client's offices. This was a case of non firmly planned project in the beginning. In the initiation phase we had to re-plan many times. Scope changed dramatically when it was no need to do any programming on the mainframe system (this activity was assigned to other seller, we simply had to interface with them). The two mainframe experts were still necessary, but they were not critical resources anymore.

I maybe didn't communicate them well this change in requirements. They thought the client was wrong, and I also was wrong allowing changing initial planning. There were other necessary project activities which demanded their expert judgment, but I didn't get them focused on any work different from what was initially planned.

Regarding the relationship with the Java team, it simply did not exist. Mainframe team had lunch at different hours. Java team members were constantly criticizing these two, etc.

---

[5] A mainframe is a high end computer by IBM with a proprietary operating system, used primarily by large organizations for critical applications, bulk data and transaction processing, much extended until 1990s before being replaced by open systems like Unix, Windows and Linux.

The problem exploded when the resource manager for them, belonging to other business unit of my company, wanted to invoice 100% of the time sheets, for a work whose net value was null. There was a lot of emails, complaints, reprimands, bad communication and in the end, everything I had written down about them was in their email boxes. There they were, the next day, waiting for me at the corridor of the client's building.

I cannot recall the two hour confrontation very well. Mi position was that two high profile professionals like them have to be in my project. They could change; adapt themselves to the new requirements. I could also make the Java team make room for them. If I asked them, they would also change (as you can see, back then I conceded more importance to Technology than to Sociology). The next day there was another two hour long discussion. This time the three of us ended up worse tempered. At the end of that week, fortunately for all, for other reasons, the client decided to get out of scope everything related to *mainframe*. The next Monday, these two people were out of my team.

I think that today I will not make the same mistakes:

- I should have not smoothed the conflict. I should have confronted the problem at the very beginning, directly with them. I should have not dealt with the problem so late, when it exploded. Escalating the problem to their boss was a big mistake. I did not apply the principle of *honesty*.

- I should have not tolerated the lack of respect inside the team. I must admit I was keener to the Java team, my lifelong team. Within the same project there should not be two separate teams. I was not *fair*.

- I should have used the resources entrusted to me in a more *responsible* way. I should have not allowed they waste their valuable time in my project, just in case they were needed.

The right decision, that corresponding to the situation for the sake of the project, was to release as soon as possible those two experts. I should have taken this decision proactively, not being acted upon by other people or circumstances. I should have decided taking into consideration all aspects involved and what is best for the project.

> *Effective Project Managers take their Effective Decisions applying Principles and considering every aspect involved within the Project*

I know this decision would have been most effective because it would be based on principles with predictable long-term results:

- The results would have been better for all directly involved, for the client and for my company. I would also have improved as an effective person, reinforcing my scale of values.
- In the end, I got the bad feeling that I dismissed these people, that I got rid of them. This would have been totally different if we have solved the problem together. My relationship with them would have been better, from then on.
- Instead of having a painful experience, I would have felt comfortable about my decision.

Old Paradigm Centered Project Management

There are many Project Managers stuck to *industrial age* paradigms, which are not principle centered. These paradigms are ineffective to manage projects in an interdependent environment. They may be effective if our business consisted of "making and selling cheeseburgers": *More people working more time produce more cheeseburgers.*

> *We must not manage projects with the industrial era mindset. Managing projects is not like "producing cheeseburgers"*

Here we are an incomplete list of obsolete Project Management Paradigms[6]:

- Paradigm #1: Bureaucracy
- Paradigm #2: Defensive Management
- Paradigm #3: Phony Deadlines (Parkinson's Law)
- Paradigm #4: Take a hard line about people goofing off on the job
- Paradigm #5: The People Store
- Paradigm #6: Multitasking (splitting people into projects)
- Paradigm #7: Steady-State Production Thinking
- Paradigm #8: Standardize Procedure (do everything by the book)
- Paradigm #9: Can Do Thinking
- Paradigm #10: The Quality-Reduced Product

---

[6] This compilation of paradigms is mainly based on three books by Tom DeMarco: Peopleware, Slack and Waltzing with bears.

Paradigm #1: Bureaucracy

There is a depressing modern trend to make team members more and more into bureaucrats. Mindless paper pushing is a waste. It ought to be attacked because it keeps people from working.

On the other side, bureaucracy hurts team formation. The team needs to believe project goals are important to the performing organization. Just telling your people that the goal matters won't be enough if you also have to tell them they should spend a third of their time pushing paper.

> *If team members devote too much time to bureaucracy tasks, they will not work as a true, goal oriented team*

Paradigm #2: Defensive Management

Project Managers that do not trust their own people are afraid they might deliver something that is wrong to the client. They are worried that mistakes may reflect badly on them. Only their own judgment is competent; they are more experienced and have a higher standard of excellence. At any point in the project where they don't interpose their own judgment, team members are more likely to make a mistake. So what? Let them make some mistakes. That doesn't mean you can't override a decision (very occasionally) or give specific direction to the project. But if the staff comes to believe it's not allowed to make any errors of its own, the message that you don't trust them comes through loud and clear. There is no message you can send that will better inhibit team formation.

Most Project Managers follow the basic premise that their people may operate completely autonomously, as long as they operate correctly. This amounts to no autonomy at all. The only freedom that has any meaning is the freedom to proceed differently from your boss. The right to be right is irrelevant; it's only the right to be wrong that makes you free. If the Project Manager interferes in any technical decision or prescribes a methodology applicable to each task, then the team won't feel trusted, and will have little inclination to bond together into a cooperative team.

> *It's only the right to be wrong that makes you free*

Paradigm #3: Phony Deadlines (Parkinson's Law)

Imagine a sensible project duration estimation of 10 months. As Project Manager knows about Parkinson's Law, which states that *work expands so as to fill the time available for its completion*, he may be tempted to reduce the time objective to 8 months, for instance. The problem appears when that goal of 8 moths is impossible to achieve and everybody knows that. The work has been defined in such a way that success is impossible. Team members will not be challenged by the goal and most important: they will not feel trusted by their boss.

> *If you reduce a sensible deadline of 10 month to a phony one of 8, chances are that you don't meet the deadline on month 8, 10, 12...*

Paradigm #4: Take a hard line about people goofing off on the job

Many Project Managers (McGregor's X theory followers), think they need to control team members tightly and make them feel a constant pressure, since the beginning of the project. They consider themselves better managers as more hours they get from the team (unpaid hours, of course). They feel satisfied when team is working some weekends.

What about if those team members love their work? Controlling how much is a team member working every time, might make sense for fast food cheeseburger production, for instance, but not for any effort for which people do the work with their minds rather than with their hands. Keeping the pressure on can make people stay focused and work harder, but don't get them work better: they just work faster.

Some studies prove that above 120 hours per week, net production is even negative (effective work is less than rework). There is a range of optimal productivity between 60-80 hours per week, but nobody can really work much more than forty hours, at least not continually and with the level of intensity required for creative work. People under pressure don't think any faster.

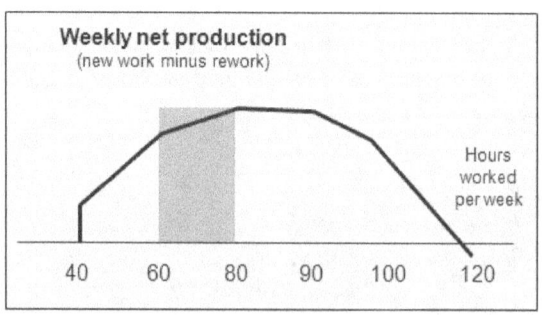

Working more than 80 hours a week does not improve productiity

Short bursts of pressure and even overtime may be a useful tactic as they focus people and increase the sense that the work is important, but extended pressure is always a counterproductive mistake.

There might be some benefit in a few extra hours worked on Saturday to meet a Monday deadline, but that's almost always followed by an equal period of compensatory *undertime* while the workers catch up with their lives. Throughout the effort there will be more or less an hour of *undertime* for every hour of overtime. The trade-off might work to the manager's advantage for the short term, but for the long term it will cancel out. Just as the unpaid overtime was largely invisible to the Project Manager (who always counts the week as forty hours regardless of how much time the people put in), so too is the *undertime* invisible. You never see it on anybody's time sheet. It's time spent on the phone or in bull sessions or just resting.

Overtime is like sprinting: It makes some sense for the last hundred meters of the marathon for those with any energy left, but if you start sprinting in the first kilometer, you're just wasting time. Trying to get people to sprint too much can only result in loss of respect for the Project Manager. The best workers have been through it all before; they know enough to keep silent and roll their eyes while the Project Manager raves on that the job has got to get done by April. Then they take their compensatory *undertime* when they can, and end up putting in forty hours of real work each week.

Terrible suspicion: The real reason for use of pressure and overtime may be to make everyone look better if the project fails.

> *The real reason for a Project Manager to use of pressure and overtime may be to make everyone look better if the project fails*

Paradigm #5: The People Store

This old paradigm, highly present nowadays thanks to globalization, consists of thinking of people as parts of the machine. The replacement part is interchangeable with the original. When a part wears out, you get another. You order a new one, more or less, by number.

Many Project Managers adopt this production environment attitude. They go to great lengths to convince themselves that no one is irreplaceable. Because they fear that a key person will leave, they force themselves to believe that there is no such thing as a key person. They act as though there were a magical People Store they could call up and say, "Send me a new Luisa Perez, but make him a little less uppity. Thank you."

Quite the opposite, a project *needs* key people. If not present at the beginning, they will become key people shortly. An Effective Project Manager encourages and welcomes this kind of personal development. For sure, he or she knows very well that replacing Luisa by Rafael has a cost.

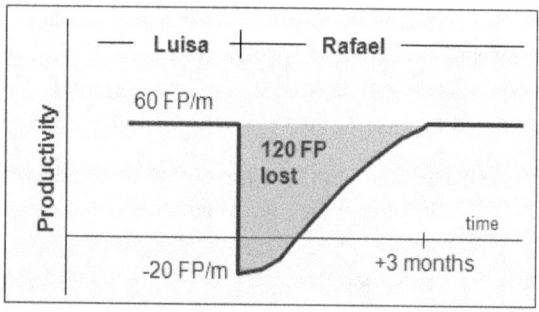

Production loss due to turnover

In the best case, if Rafael comes a day after the departure of Luisa, he will start producing that day, but with a negative net productivity. Let's say Luisa's productivity for this software project was measured as 60 Function Points a month. Rafael is not yet familiar with the project, so he needs help from teammates, and he makes many mistakes and rework. Let's say initial Rafael's productivity is about -20 FP/month. His productivity rate will increase linearly until he gets so productive as Luisa.

The shaded area of the figure (resembling a triangle) represents graphically the cost of replacement. He takes 3 month to get Luisa's productivity level, this cost is more than 120 FP. In this example, we can say that replacing Luisa by Rafael costs us 2 as much as 2 months of Luisa. And that's in the best case. It's easy to imagine the higher impact when replacement is not there the following day (the shaded area will be a kind of rectangle + triangle).

> *Team Members are not interchangeable*
> *pieces of a machine*

Paradigm #6: Multitasking (Splitting People into Projects)

Some Project Managers think their team members are so skillful and experts than they impose a fragmentation of time policy for them. So these valuable professionals are split into several projects apart of their main assignation.

Fragmentation is bad for team formation, but it's also bad for efficiency. People can keep track of only so many human interactions.

When they try to be part of four working groups, they have four times as many interactions to track. They spend all their time changing gears.

No one can be part of multiple synergic teams. The tight interactions of the synergic team are exclusive. Enough fragmentation and teams just won't synergize. The saddest thing is we allow far more fragmentation than is really necessary. We tend to concede this battle without even a fight. Simply saying that a goal is to assign people only one piece of work at a time can result in significant reductions of fragmentation, and thus give teams a real chance to form.

> *No one can be part of multiple synergic cohesive teams*

Paradigm #7: Steady-State Production Thinking

A Project Manager could estimate and manage his project assuming a constant productivity rate (not rising, nor decreasing). Project productivity rate can be measured in many ways: releases per week, functionality built or documentation produced per day per person, etc.

However, projects are dynamic systems. Projects are not repetitive operations. Steady-state production thinking is particularly ill-suited to project work. Project's entire purpose is to put itself out of business. The only steady state in the life of a project is *rigor mortis*. Unless you are about to close or cancel, the entire focus of project management ought to be the dynamics of the development effort. You have to pay attention to how well each of the team members fit into the effort as a whole.

> *The only steady state in the life of a project is rigor mortis*

Paradigm #8: Standardize Procedure (do everything by the book)

Project Managers don't manage in isolation, they manage inside a performing organization, meaning they have to apply organizational process assets and take into account enterprise environmental factors.

Doing everything by the book may give good results in operation management, but it hardly does in project management. Projects have a very unique nature. They are prone to unclassified problems, unanticipated issues, innovation, cultural shock, drama, luck, etc.

Project Managers are grateful to have available management processes, templates, mandatory deliverables, good practices, process frameworks, methodologies, etc. *All a Project Manager may need is already invented.* However, in the moment of truth, what counts is to deliver on time, on cost, with the required functionality and acceptable quality. These are the primary goals. The end justifies the means.

When managing projects, the need of *thinking* on the job, not just *doing* it, is also important for team formation. The activities planned for the team generally don't include a provision of "unproductive" time for planning, investigating new methods, training, reading books, estimating, budgeting, scheduling, and allocating personnel, etc.

Typical industrial era mindset concedes no importance to "think about the job". If you are charged with getting a task done, what proportion of your time ought to be dedicated to actually doing the task? Not one hundred percent. The inclination is to push the effort into one hundred percent do-mode. If an excuse is needed for the lack of think-time, the excuse is always time pressure (as though there were ever work to be done without time pressure).

The key question "ought this thing to be done at all?" is more relevant for critical projects. The more heroic the effort required, the more important it is that the team members learn to interact well and enjoy it. The project that has to be done by an impossible fixed date is the very one that can't afford not to have frequent brainstorms and even a project dinner or some such affair to help the individual participants knit into an effective whole.

> *Following Standard Procedures is good for Operations*
> *It is not necessarily good for Projects*

Paradigm #9: Can Do Thinking

Your boss asks you to consider taking on a project that has to be done by Christmas, with only 3 people available to work on int. You express doubts that there is enough time to get the software built. "That's why I picked you to manage the job".

You'll get the job, the challenge, and the prestige ... But you'll have to believe in the schedule, that's the price to pay. You swallow hard and say you'll do it. Later, you bolster your belief. Sure, why not Christmas? Other projects have accomplished as much in as little time, haven't they?

Before long, you may find yourself actually felling confident. Time will for sure prove otherwise, but for the moment, you are practically sure you can get the job done. Yes, that's what you believe, but do you have any right to believe it? Without knowing it, you have fallen in "Can Do" Thinking.

Staring your boss in the face and saying January 1 when you know that even three months later would be optimistic sounds bad. It sounds like lying. But being a "Can Do" manager sounds good. We're all expected to have a certain Can Do attitude.

Let's admit it: We feel a little thrill of approval when the big boss calls for extraordinary performance and subordinates respond: "We can do this. That's a great idea, boss. We'll get right on it." This is the expected submission and acceptance of challenges. We tell ourselves: "Nobody would ever do anything ambitious if they didn't commit to do it, no matter how undoable it sounds at the beginning." Can Do thinking is a fixture in most modern companies.

Can Do Thinking is, unfortunately, antithetical to effective project management. Effective Project Managers have to acknowledge directly the Can't Do possibilities and to approach *what they don't have the right* to believe as risks to be explicitly managed.

> *Your boss is expecting you "Can Do" but...*
> *Do you have the right to believe you can?*
>
> *Project Managers should better think "Can't do"*
> *(what they don't have the right to believe)*

Paradigm #10: The Quality-Reduced Product

Nobody really talks about quality-reduced products. What they talk about is cost-reduced products. But it usually boils down to the same thing. The typical steps we take to deliver a product in less time result in lower quality. Often the product's end user gives willing consent to this trade-off (less quality for earlier, cheaper delivery).

But such concessions can be very painful for the team members. Their self-esteem and enjoyment are undermined by the necessity of building a product of clearly lower quality than what they are capable of.

An early casualty of quality reduction is whatever sense of team identification the group has been able to build. Co-workers who are developing a shoddy product don't even want to look each other in the eye. There is no joint sense of accomplishment in store for them. They know that there will be a general sense of relief when they can stop doing what they're doing. At the end of the project, they'll make every effort to separate themselves from other members of the group, and get on to better things.

All team members understand that work quality is important to the organization, but synergic teams adopt higher levels of quality to distinguish themselves. Without that distinctive sign the team is just a group, not a true team.

> *Co-workers who are developing a shoddy product don't even want to look each other in the eye*

The Project Manager's Essential Body Parts

In his bestselling book *The Deadline*[7], Tom DeMarco describes the most important parts of the "anatomy" of any Project Manager: gut, heart, soul and nose. According to Tom DeMarco, good Project Managers must develop a habit of trusting their "gut", leading with the "heart", building "soul" into the organization and last, but not least, to have a "nose" capable of smelling problems.

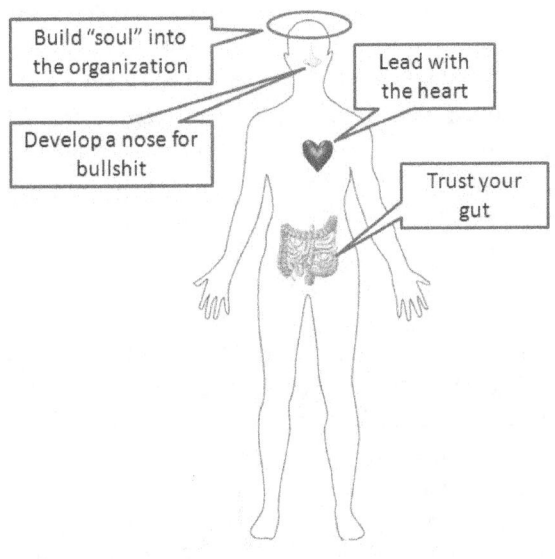

---

[7] The Deadline: A Novel About Project Management, Tom DeMarco, Dorset House Publishing, 1997. Chapter 6. The world's greatest project manager.

- **Trust your gut** (follow your natural instinct): You consider someone for a key position and he or she looks fine on paper, but something tells you to keep on looking. That's something is your gut. And then someone else comes along, and a little voice inside you sings out, "This is the guy!" or "She is the one! Grab her and put her in charge of the whole works and leave her alone". That's the gut speaking. The best managers are the ones with the best guts. The key brain function a manager has to master is to learn when to trust her gut.

- **Lead with the heart**: It's your heart that people respond to. They don't follow you because you're clever or because you're always right, but because they love you. The heady leader can lead, but people won't follow. Maybe you have to be born to it.

- **Build "soul" into the organization**: Project prosper to the extent that people learn to work together effectively. If they worked entirely apart, then soul wouldn't matter. Management would be a simple matter of coordinating their efforts, a mechanical process. Real work requires close, warm, and almost intimate interconnections between team members, and easy, effective, interaction through the whole organization. You don't make it happen at all. You let it happen. You create an atmosphere where it can happen. And then, if you're lucky, it does happen. You get them to think about integrity and all the baggage that word carries. It has to be some shared vision that unifies the group. The human creature has a need to be part of a community. An amazing number of today's people don't even know their neighbors. Community doesn't come from our towns anymore. But the need for community is still in us. For most of us, the best chance of a community is at work.

- **Develop a nose for bullshit**: There are plenty of problems in every project. Preparing the proper response in advance sometimes makes the difference between life and death for a Project Manager. The experienced Project Manager is used to smell the problems from far away.

A Character Ethic for the Project Manager

To explain the essence of effectiveness, Covey reminds us the Aesop's fable of *The Goose and the Golden Egg*: A farmer discovers one day that one of his pet gooses has delivered a pure golden egg. Day after day he finds a new golden egg and becomes fabulously wealthy. But with his increasing wealth comes greed and impatience. In order to *produce more with less*, he kills the goose to get the all golden eggs at once. But when he opens the goose, he finds it empty.

When he sacrificed the goose, he destroyed the production capacity. That was a mistake: What he should have done was to feed and take care of the goose. The essence of effectiveness in natural systems is based on balancing two things: what is Produced (P = the golden eggs) and the producing asset or Production Capacity (PC = the goose). You always reap what you sow. It's the Law of the Harvest.

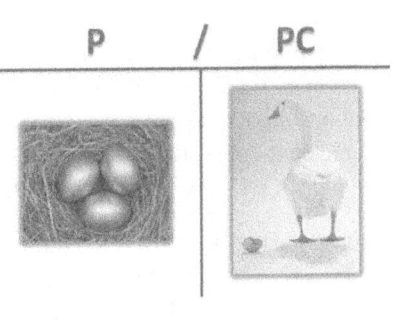

People must develop continuously as complete persons but at the same time they need to cover their vital needs. Private companies must invest on their employees and customer care, but at the same time they need to produce and to sell. Analogously, Project Managers must forge a character of principles (throughout good habits), invest in their continuous learning and professional network, but at the same time they need to achieve the project goals.

> *Projects are Natural Systems: They follow the Law of the Harvest*

3. Project Manager must be a "Good Person"

Did you ever consider how ridiculous it would be to try to cram on a farm -- to forget to plant in the spring, play all summer and then cram in the fall to bring in the harvest? The farm is a natural system. The price must be paid and the process followed. You always reap what you sow; there is no shortcut.

Think for instance in the case of "studying the day before the exam". In the short run, in an artificial social system such as school, you may be able to get by if you learn how to manipulate the man-made rules, to "play the game". In most one-shot or short-lived human interactions, you can use the *personality ethic* to get by and to make favorable impressions through charm and skill and pretending to be interested in other people's hobbies. You can pick up quick, easy techniques that may work in short-term situations. But secondary traits alone have no permanent worth in long-term relationships. Eventually, if there isn't deep integrity and fundamental character strength, the challenges of life will cause true motives to surface and human relationship failure will replace short-term success.

This principle is also true, ultimately, in human behavior, in human relationships that we can have in Projects. They, too, are natural systems based on The Law of the Harvest. There is a team that you don't know if it is going to form. There is a product that you don't know if will be due on time, on cost, with the required functionality. There are so many factors that can influence goal achievements.

Project Management is not a science. You cannot aspire to the deterministic control you could have in operation management. Long term project management effectiveness has to be based on good habits.

A character of effectiveness can be formed with 7 habits, according to Covey:

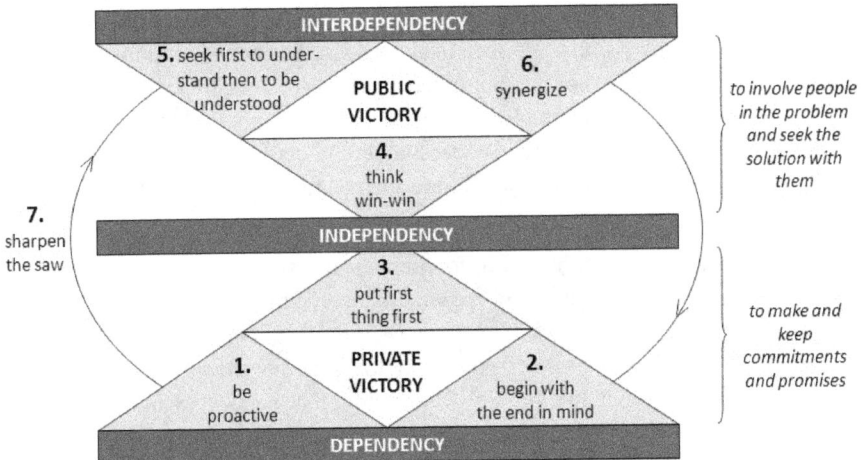

Effectiveness cannot be imposed from outside. You change only if you want (change door is open from inside). There is a sequential path inside-out, from dependence to interdependence:

- You cannot be effective if you are **dependent**: Private victory precedes public victory. First you need to be independent: you are not affected by environment, you are self-confident. You have to be effective by yourself, to make and keep commitments and promises. This means **proactivity, planning** and **execution**. An Independent Project Manager keeps documentation updated. We see him managing *gantts*, monitoring and controlling activities assigned to team members, keeping documents up to date, etc.

▪ Being effective in an **interdependent** environment comes after. An Independent Project Manager may burn the team out, reach win-lose agreements with stakeholders, ignore the real requirements, quality criteria, needed changes, etc. Every knowledge worker, especially Project Managers, work in an inter-dependent environment. Projects don't fail usually for technical reasons, but social reasons. Public victory consists of making others do what we need by themselves, for their own initiative. But we need that not only for today, but for tomorrow. This demands investing emotionally on others. You have to be good in **negotiation, communication** and **leadership**.

▪ Finally, we need renewal, to **sharpen the saw**. We frequently don't have time to planning, preparation, prevention and empowerment. We are *too busy driving to have time to get gas*. While you are executing the project, you need to think on the process you are following, not just blindly follow. Since projects start to finish, we have to grow as complete persons, not just in a fragment of our live, but integrally in our four intelligences: body, mind, heart and spirit. An Effective Project Manager must invest in his professional network, especially on team members' *emotional bank account*. In the future there will be more projects with them. He must to learn from his own mistakes. He must organize the acquired knowledge. He must look for greater challenges. He must be ready to **perform better the next project**.

The Habits of Effective Project Managers

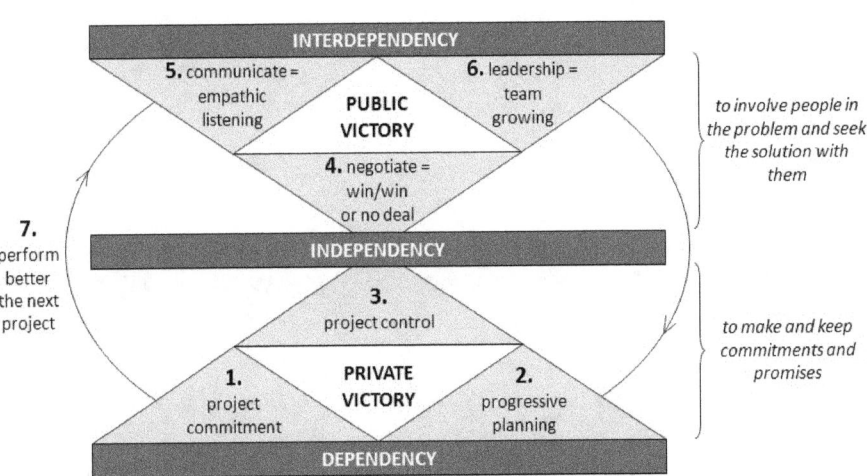

To learn and not to do is really not to learn
To know and not to do is really not to know

STEPHEN R. COVEY

4. The Habits of Effective Project Managers

This chapter (the central part of this book) is aimed to develop a structured model of the personal skills that, in my opinion, a Project Manager needs in order to be effective.

As you can see later on in Appendix I. Performance Appraisal for Project Managers, PMI has already produced a standard on personal skills entitled Project Manager Competency Development Framework. For many reasons that you also could read there, in my humble opinion, I do not think this could be an easy model to put into practice, when appraising or improving personal skills of Project Managers. Conversely, many people have used the 7 Habits Covey's model for more than two decades, in their path to effectiveness. The 7 Habits framework has been adapted to families, teenagers, schools and corporations, always exceeding all expectations.

If somebody needs effectiveness more than anyone, this is the Project Manager. Very few professions are more objective oriented than Project Management. As effective people, Project Managers should follow the 7 Habits Covey's paradigm, and of course, his whole advice to seek our voice and inspire others at work, principle-centered leadership, personal planning, etc. This could be necessary, but I think it is not sufficient.

> *We could learn, teach and practice 7 Habits Covey's model using the language of our profession*

Following, there is a proposed matching between the 7 Habits Covey's model and the habits a Project Manager should be proficient in.

4. The Habits of Effective Project Managers

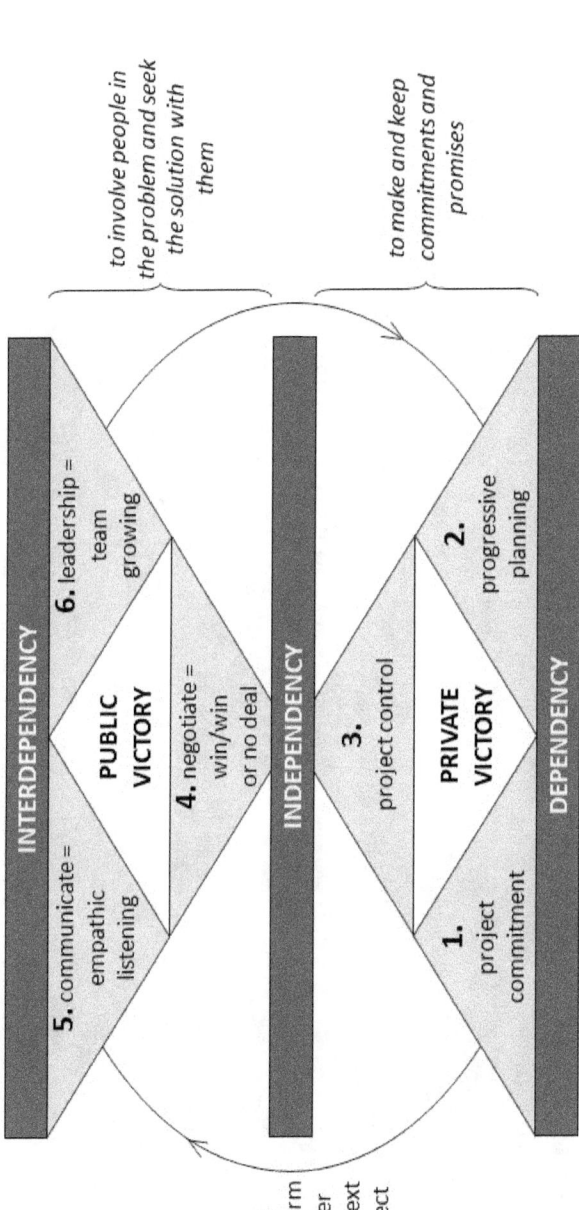

Figure 1: The Habits of Effective Project Managers

The 7 Habits of Highly Effective People

The Habits of Effective Project Managers

character ethic / code of ethics and professional conduct	#	Habit	PM Habit	
private victory = to make and keep commitments and promises	1	be proactive	project commitment	1.1 I plan my project 1.2 I make and keep promises 1.3 I fight for my people
	2	begin with the end in mind	progressive planning	2.1 I visualize destiny and path 2.2 I keep an updated and credible plan 2.3 I can say no
	3	put first things first	project control	3.1 I wear my executive cap 3.2 I control baselines 3.3 I use PM tools
public victory = to involve people in the problem and seek the solution with them	4	think win/win	negotiate = win/win or no deal	4.1 Win/win or no deal with clients and sellers 4.2 Win/win or no deal with team conflicts 4.3 Win/win or no deal with risks
	5	seek first to understand, then to be understood	communicate = empathic listening	5.1 With people, slow is fast 5.2 I manage expectations 5.3 I adapt my communication to stakeholders
	6	sinergize	leadership = team growing	6.1 I adapt my leadership to situation 6.2 I manage people by objectives 6.3 I appreciate the differences
self-renewal	7	sharpen the saw	perform better the next project	7.1 Yesterday's problems are today's risks 7.2 Self-appraisal 7.3 Growing my network

Table 1: Matching the Habits of Highly Effective People to Project Managers

4.1 Habit 1. Committing to the Project

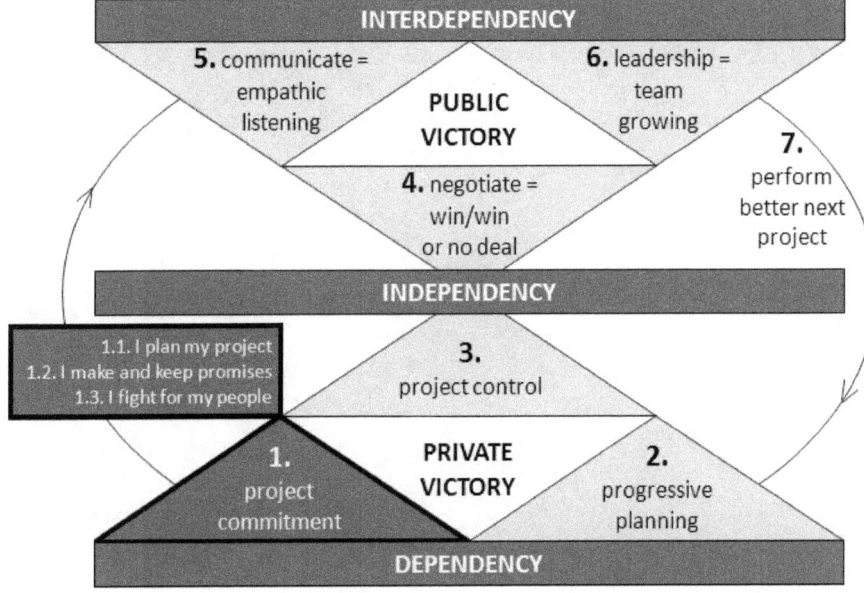

There is a gap between stimulus and response and the key to both our growth and happiness is how we utilize that space

VIKTOR E. FRANKL

4. The Habits of Effective Project Managers

The 1ˢᵗ Habit of Effective People: Be Proactive

The first habit of highly effective people, according to Covey is "be proactive". This is the first habit you need to overcome the initial stage of maturity, when we are "dependent. You cannot aspire to be effective if you are affected by everything that happens outside. If you have a bad day just because it rains, you cannot be independent. Independent people can carry *their own weather* with them. Whether it rains or shines makes no difference to them. They recognize their control zone and play within. People are not like animals. Animals are reactive: they always react to stimulus the same way, as programmed by instinct or training.

According to Covey, people have 4 human gifts that make us different from animals:

- **Imagination**: The ability to create in our minds beyond our present reality.
- **Self-Awareness**: We human beings are aware of ourselves. Self-awareness is the ability to do what you just did is uniquely human. the ability to think about your very thought process
- **Independent Will**: The ability to act based on our self-awareness, free of all other influences.
- **Conscience**: A deep inner awareness of right and wrong, of the principles that govern our behavior, and a sense of the degree to which our thoughts and actions are in harmony with them.

When you are proactive, you don't react to stimulus automatically. According to Covey, responsibility is the ability to choose your response[8]. There is a gap between stimulus and response. As human beings, we can choose freely the best response to any stimulus, using our 4 human gifts.

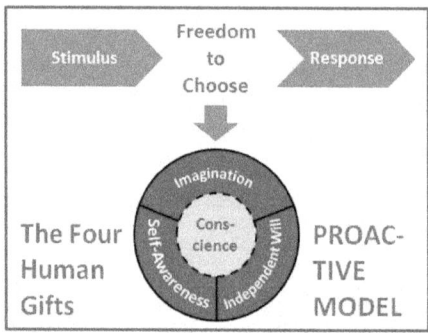

People can program their response to any stimulus. We can be proactive by taking distance from the stimulus and emotion, taking time and space to find the optimal solution and respond accordingly. There is a big difference between response and reaction. We humans can choose our response because we are not animals. On the other hand, because we are not animals, we may be conditioned by our reactive language (and again we don't take any advantage of our human condition):

- *What an awful day!*
- *He has not had 5 minutes to call me be back!*
- *She forgot our date!*

---

[8] Notice the word pun: responsibility = response-ability.

How different it will be the effect that language could have in us if we would use a factual language, taking distance of stimulus and emotion:

- *It is raining.*
- *He didn't call.*
- *I was there, she didn't.*

Covey advised us to "listen our own language". *We see the world not as it is, but as we are.* Sometimes, being proactive is so simple as discovering that we are using a reactive language.

> *We see the world not as it is, but as we are*

We can exercise our human freedom to choose by applying the 4 human gifts. We can see the matching between the 4 human gifts and the complete person paradigm:

- **Imagination** is related with **the mind**: The ability to use our mind to see another different reality.
- **Self-Awareness** is related with **the heart**: It has to do with the emotional intelligence, the ability to empathize, to relate to others.
- **Independent Will** is related with **the body**: Our ability to discipline our body to do what we decide.
- **Conscience** is related with **the spirit**: Our spiritual intelligence is that inner voice (the voice of conscience) which tell us what is right and wrong.

The most dramatic example of these 4 human gifts in action is the experience of Viktor Frankl, related in his autobiographical book *Man's search for meaning*[9]. Viktor Frankl was Jewish psychiatrist. In his book he narrates his Second War experience in Auschwitz's Nazi death camps, after having lost his wife, siblings and parents.

In this awful situation, with the permanent feeling that he was going to be killed by any nuisance in the next few minutes, Viktor should have felt very close to the "animal state". He should have not thought with logic and rationale. In this situation, precisely, Viktor Frankl grew up and found his greatness and his life's meaning:

- **Imagination**: He used his imagination to invent a new school in psychology, called logotherapy. He projected himself into lecturing to his students after his release from the death camps. Thanks to his powerful imagination, he felt many times freer than his German jailers.

- **Self-Awareness**: He observed his own thoughts. He could situate as viewer of himself, when jailers insulted him or when his mates asked him for advice.

- **Independent Will**: In times of collective despair, when maybe he needed more help than the others, he chose to put light as psychotherapist to his mates. Without any doubt, we can say that some of his speeches saved the lives of many.

- **Conscience**: He transformed his experience of grief into an experience of spiritual growth, self-transcendence, contribution and meaning.

---

[9] Man's search for meaning, Viktor E. Frankl, Ed. Herder.

The 1st Habit of Effective Project Managers: Project Commitment

You won't be an Effective Project Manager if you are overwhelmed by your physical or emotional environment. You are not going to deliver a good product or result if you are always complaining about your company, about the scarce resources, the project constraints, how poorly sold and badly staffed your project was, how immature is your organization on project management, how hard is to use corporate tools, excessive bureaucracy, lack of management support, etc. You may be right on each complaint, but first thing is your project, and your project is severely damaged if you lead and manage from a reactive mindset. Moreover, I cannot demonstrate it, but I'm sure of this: *You will not have good luck.*

Like it or not, the project is there. It has to be a success and you have been appointed in charge. This is a fact, and you don't solve anything denying this reality. First thing an Effective Project Manager has to do is accepting the role. Even if you are not being empowered with the desirable level of authority, you have to act as if you were. You keep in mind that, in the end, if the project is late, has a cost overrun, or many client complaints, then you are going to be judged responsible, *as if you had been empowered with total authority.*

You are effective as a Project Manager only if you are truly committed. If a Project Manager believes he can be successful even if the project is a failure, this means that he does not understand at all his role as a Project Manager. In the project you are managing right now, please ask yourself a question:

> *If my project is the bacon-and-egg breakfast,*
> *what role am I playing: Chicken or Pig?*

As Project Managers, we are judged mostly by our performance in goal achievement. Therefore, we need to make the project goals our personal goals. If a project has been poorly sold, you should elaborate a new version of the plan. You should always work with a realistic and feasible plan.

If that is not the case, if they oblige you to work with a plan which is not feasible, you should meet the sponsor and tell him, for instance: "As of today, with the information we have, after estimation work involving expert judgment, I cannot ensure the delivery date in 5 months with a team of 10 team members full time. I can't neither guarantee you a finance margin of 20%; let me demonstrate you why…"

But you don't stuck on the complaint phase; please continue your meeting proposing reasonable solutions: "I've thought these three alternatives in order to work with a realistic plan…"

This ability to take commitments, to decide to wear our "Project Manager cap", has to be translated into habits. The first habit of highly effective people "be proactive", could be translated as the generic habit of 1) Project Commitment and other three specific sub-habits: 1.1) I do plan my project; 1.2) I make and keep promises and 1.3) I fight for my people.

Here are some typical phrases that reflect our behavior when we incorporate these habits in our character:

1.1) I do plan my project:

- "According to the contract, the Project is due in 5 months. Unfortunately I was not involved in the bidding phase. I need to elaborate this initial plan so that it looks realistic, only then I could commit with the goals. I'll justify the changes I may need to introduce in the next steering committee meeting."

1.2) I make and keep promises:

- "The Project will deliver this release between April the 20th and Mach the 10th."

- "If this risk occurs, after applying the response plan, we will have a slippage of 5 days, no more."

1.3) I fight for my people:

- "I want Martha in my project. I'm sorry but I'm not counting with Ivan because the project will be resented".

- "I need George. These activities depend much on him. I know you count on him on March. I've talked with the resource manager and you could have these alternatives instead…"

1.1) I Do Plan my Project

The firs symptom of a Project Manager who is not proactive is that he does not have an updated credible plan. That is, he does not know what is going to happen next week, next month, and so on. This is serious. Not just for the image as an inefficient Project Manager: lack of predictability produces low morale among team members.

There is no excuse for a Project Manager to not having a project plan (be it formally written down or just on his or her head). First to all, a plan is the main tool for a Project Manager. Secondly, that plan may be useful for other stakeholders.

If the performing organization does not have a mandatory template for project plans, then the Project Manager have to proactively propose one. There are many templates available, you don't need to invent here —all a Project Manager may need is already invented. The best format will be the one covering the communication needs. It is typical a gantt chart, but it may be sufficient a milestone chart, a to-do-list, a deliverables list, a risk list, etc.

Planning is not just to be done at the beginning. It's good practice anytime during the project. It may be even more important last weeks, when project closing is coming and deliverables have to be formally accepted on time. Best practice is to have a thorough project management plan since the beginning, agreed among stakeholders and experts, with stakeholders completely identified, with the sponsor's commitment, project justification, schedule, budget, risks, scope, milestones, activities, detailed costs, etc.

When a Project Manager struggling with day to day crisis, improvising all the time, responding to new problems and changes, then all of a sudden he raises his head and decides to take perspective, and he prepares a schedule plan, and start thinking about next things to do in the future, something shines over him.

He reminds me Neo, the main role in the film The Matrix, when he stops running and decides to fight Mr. Smith. Trinity says "What's he doing?" Morpheus responds "He's beginning to believe".

Our Project Manager could say something like this: "That's enough improvising. I do plan my project. Today I'm going to plan the activities of this week, after that I'm to plan next week…"

1.2) I Make and Keep Promises

For many managers, proactivity in Project Management stands for predictability. Day to day operations are predictable and uniforms, but a project is hardly like this. Efforts, costs, deadlines, milestones, deliveries, issues, don't distribute uniformly: there are more deliveries at the end than at the middle of the project; milestones' due dates may be delayed considerably. Most of the times, the main reason they put a Project Manager in charge is to keep reporting all these variables.

Most industrial era paradigm managers aspire to a deterministic control of the project: if they control these variables, they control the project. For this reason, those managers will often ask you your best cost and duration estimates for a given activity. They will take note, and when the due date is close or when the actual cost is reaching a threshold, they will come and ask you again.

The project may have changed scope so much, it could still be suffering from key resource scarcity, it may have suffered a lot of unpredictable issues and many risks have materialized, but for them, the only thing that counts is that you are going to meet the deadline or the budget for that activity, so as you promised. What activity? You may even get the project rid of that activity. "Wake up, Neo. The Matrix has you".

As a Project Manager, what does the word *proactivity* mean for you? It means *you make your own promises*. You don't need others make commitments on your behalf. The habit of making and keeping promises is the first step to effectiveness. You don't depend on what happen outside, you are not dependent. You are the programmer. You can truly commit. But you take care of what you promise, because you have to keep your promises.

Effective Project Managers don't make absolute promises. They should indicate the range of possible results. Remember: without +/- it's not an estimate. When due date is six months far, it doesn't sound professional to say that activity is going to finish March the 26th sharp. What if they ask in the morning or afternoon? You should say, for instance "That activity will finish between March 19th and April the 6th". If we promise something for next week the uncertainty window will be smaller, of course.

> *Without +/- it's not an estimate*

1.3) I Fight for My People

When I was preparing for the PMP® exam, I was surprised when I found out that process *6.3 Estimate Activity Resources* (a planning process where I say, for instance, that I need 2,5 programmers and 0,75 database administrators) is separated from the process *9.2 Acquire Project Team* (an executing process where I have to know the names of the people I need. Up to then, I always thought these two processes were performed at once: "I will need a 50% of Mike and Mary full-time". PMBOK® showed me this was not good practice. Instead, I have to say that it will be Mike (not John) and Mary (not Peter) not at the beginning, but when the project is executing.

4. The Habits of Effective Project Managers

This made me think that acquiring the team was not a one-shot activity, but a progressive one, demanding a lot of effort from the Project Manager. As expressed in PMBOK, process groups may overlap: Execution and planning overlap when I say "This activity has to be done by Mike in order to last only 15 days". Execution and initiating overlap when I say "Mary is a key critical resource for the success of this project".

Nowadays, after many projects and experiences, process 9.2 looks to me like the most important out of the 42 processes in PMBOK version 4th. I've learned this also from the Project Managers I've worked for, when they fought for me. When I started working, I heard a joke about me: "I'll have Jose on my team. Someone whose surname is Barato has to be good for the project, ha, ha, ha". This joke was not very funny to me. So, when I was assigned to a new project, my obsession was to show I was valuable. I wanted they tell of me things like: "I'll have Jose on my team because after a few days, he's managing the project by himself". I think I got it, because when I finished a project, there were many offers to me. They invited me to lunch, talked about "my professional career", "my progress within the firm", "new challenges", blah, blah, blah.

I recall there was a small office where they met in order to decide on project staffing. If you were close, you could hear how they argue about you:

"[...] I happen to talk to Barato the other day [...] He's very interested in this line of business of mine [...] I gave him to you last time, now it's my turn [...] I can share a 15% of him, but no more [...] So you have to accept he is mine, you find another, it's not my problem!"

When my time was over, then they started with another colleague. This kind of gossip had a big effect on our egos, but at the same time we wondered "These guys... what's the problem with them? One day they are going to kill each other! Why do they think that project success is a thing they solve in just one meeting?" As they left the meeting, you could tell how upset the defeated one was. When you crossed him, he didn't even say hello!

The Habits of Effective Project Managers | 75

Conversely, the winner came to you with a big smile on his face and told you the good news: "You are on my project, Jose. I bet for you, so please don't let me down!"

If you are a Project Manager, you have to know you cannot protect yourself against your own people's incompetence. If your staff isn't up to the job at hand, you will fail. As a Project Manager, you totally depend on your team. You don't do the work, your team do. You just decide what people do when. In a sense, you are like an orchestra director, you don't play the instruments. At the very beginning, you may perform some tasks in some detail, but your goal is to focus on pure management, and you will be able to do that only when your team is formed, synergic and self-sufficient. But you cannot produce a formed team. You don't make it happen, you let it happen. It depends totally on them. Of course, if the people are badly suited to the job, you should get new people. But once you've decided to go with a given group, your best tactic is to trust them.

> *If your staff isn't up to the job at hand,*
> *you will fail*

4.2 Habit 2. Planning Progressively

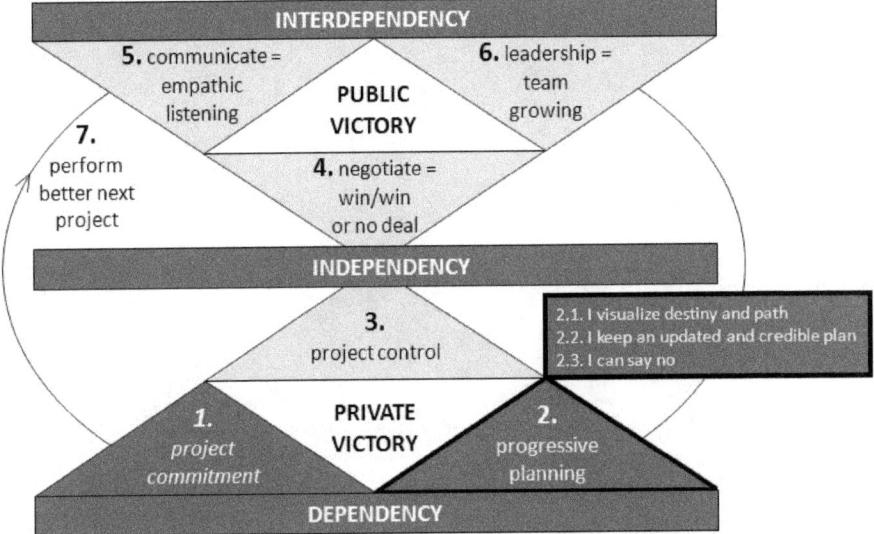

What is now proved was once only imagined

WILLIAM BLAKE

*In times of crisis, only imagination
is more important than knowledge*

ALBERT EINSTEIN

4. The Habits of Effective Project Managers

The 2nd Habit of Effective People: Start with the End in Mind

The second habit of highly effective people, according to Covey is "start with the end in mind". You could not be effective if you don't visualize clearly you long term objectives in life.

Once you are proactive, you have to take effective decisions. Effective decisions are wise and balanced. As effective person, you have to considerer all your roles in live —as a worker, student, volunteer, spouse, father/mother, son/daughter, believer in God, member of a community, etc.

In order to evaluate your options, you have to take distance of situational emotion and other environmental factors. You get the best solution considering the balance whole —professional needs, family needs, and other needs involved and possible implications of alternative decisions.

Effective people keep clear vital objectives, and these objectives are based on principles. If you base your live in superficial objectives, what Covey names as "alternative centers" (as money, work, pleasure, family, possessions, friends, enemies, etc.), then you could be effective in the short term, but this kind of success usually fades out: they are external, not in our control zone, they will go as they come.

Lasting success requires visualize where do you want to get and what intermediate steps lead you closer until you get your final destiny.

If your ladder of success is leaning against the wrong wall you are efficient (you climb hard), but you are not effective. You simply would realize earlier you were following a wrong direction.

When you have clear in your mind your mission statement (how you would like to be remembered) then it is easy and quick to say "Yes!"; or to say "No!" because you have a another burning "Yes!" inside.

When you take a decision guided by your internal long term objectives, you'll feel comfortable about your decision. Whatever you choose to do, you can focus on it and enjoy it. Doing so, you reinforce your character, grow as person and, I cannot demonstrate why: *You will have good luck.*

All things are created twice. Firstly, things are real in our mind. Secondly, things are physically created. First habit says "you are the programmer", second habit says "you write the program". Second habit requires using two human gifts: imagination and conscience. With imagination you elaborate goals. With conscience you if they are right, if they are based on principles.

Effective people devote time to think about future. They visualize abstract things to imagine a future state of reality in the long term. They chose the right goals (based on principles). When taking decisions they are usually fast (and they are usually right).

The 2nd Habit of Effective Project Managers: Progressive Planning

Project Managers should accomplish the above, in the personal level. In the professional level, it is important they abide the Code of Ethics and Professional Conduct by PMI®[10]. In their day to day job, Project Managers should master the habit of visualizing about the project. Deliverables are also created twice. Before that deliverables could be tangible, the Project Manager had already imagined them. Before that team members could follow a number of processes and develop many activities, the Project Manager "had already been there". Starting with the end in mind, in the field of Project Management, means something very specific: planning.

Before insisting about the importance of good planning for every Project (*fail to plan is plan to fail*), let's think of what happen when the Project Manager doesn't have the habit of planning. When you see someone leading a project just doing what customer asks, responding day to day issues and crisis just by reacting. Can you call this to manage a project? Let's set some examples:

- A client contracts a service to have a team in his venues, leaded by a person that comes occasionally, but the day to day tasks are determined by client. Let's call this technical support, but don't call this a project. Would this client have the right to complain when deadlines or goals are not met? Should he call for a fixed price?

---

[10] Principles of responsibility, respect, fairness and honesty are adapted to Project Management in the Code of Ethics and Professional Conduct by PMI®. The document can be downloaded at http://www.pmi.org

▪ There was a technical team working together to implement a corporate tool in an organization. There was a Project Manager assigning the work, scheduling meetings, escalating issues. With many difficulties and hardly disturbing stakeholders, after many missed deadlines and setbacks, she finally got the tool implemented. She was considered a heroin. That tool was so useful that was included in a contract with a client, as part of the service. Suddenly all alarms are triggered: The client is reporting high severity issues and penalties because the tool is malfunctioning impacting the business. Now we see our Project Manager is no longer a heroin. She is a villain! Top managers start talking line like these: "On that important product development project there was no requirement management. How was that possible? Wasn't there any formal testing? Where is the scope statement? Why was no risk management at all?" The Project Manager regrets not having an approved project management plan document. Sadly she has not a good defense. She worked without a plan, reacting and improvising. As discussed in chapter 2: We are Project <u>Managers</u>, with a strong weight on the word "Managers", mainly to be blamed for failure.

▪ One software project is sold. It has been a bidding success. The sales manager is quite happy. The only problem is that the client wants the product in 6 months, not 10. After tough negotiations, an agreement is made on the same budget and effort. The Project Manager had estimated a progressive increase of the team members: only a few designers at the beginning, programmers gradually incorporating. Now he has the whole team of 10 programmers the first day. Would they all start the design phase? No, they all start programming. The design work, if performed anyhow, will be a development byproduct. Here we are another Project Manager who is working without a plan. He does his best in follow-up meetings, the client rejecting nearly every release, generating much rework.

Here we are another project not deserving that name, being managed more as operations. Would someone be surprised when the project is not finished on month 6, nor 10, but on month 12, after poor quality and widespread dissatisfaction at both sides? Notice the curious line: *The client said 6 months to push pressure on the seller (Parkinson's Law).*

A Project Manager who lacks the habit of planning is giving a bad impression. *He is not doing his job right.* He is not managing a project. He is managing other thing. When a stakeholder criticizes him in a follow-up meeting because he is continually improvising, he gets blushed.

What kind of professional image is a Project Manager giving if he doesn't know best what to be done from now on? If he prepares a *gantt* not for himself, but to look good in the follow-up meeting, this is very noticeable. He is not reporting project status. Why has he arranged this meeting? Just to get to know what to do next, I'm afraid.

How different the impression (and how effective we look!) when we are truly committed to the project (habit 1) and we have a clear image of the project future and near steps. The second habit of highly effective people "start with the end in mind" could be translated as the generic habit of <u>2) Progressive Panning</u> and other three specific sub-habits: <u>2.1) I Visualize Destiny and Path</u>; <u>2.2) I Keep an Updated Credible Plan</u> and <u>2.3) I Can Say No</u>.

Following there are some lines that flows naturally when we integrate in our character habits 1 and 2:

- **2.1) I Visualize Destiny and Path**:

  - "Affected users will need this training before week 15. Training feedback will be taken into account in change management activities."

  - "First development iteration will solve all architectural technical issues throughout a prototype. Second iteration will release all functionality for accounts receivable, which is the most critical. Third iteration will cover the remaining functionality."

  - "Testing separate team will be needed as of 5 FTE in July, 8 FTE in September and 10 FTE in January."

  - "We should negotiate the licensing terms of the project product. Our company could extend this business line with this."

- **2.2) I keep an Updated Credible Plan**:

  - "Initial assumptions are not valid anymore. Here it is the new project management plan."

  - "For the main work packages and control accounts, scheduling is as due. Here you are the next month planning for low level activities and milestones."

  - "If project is early canceled next month, these could be the scope packages ready to deliver."

  - "There is no chance of delivery before March. Best chance for acceptable product is March 31, but confidence level is low (30%).

We have to wait until April 15 to have 50% confidence. If we want to publish a deadline with sure no delay, that will be June 1":

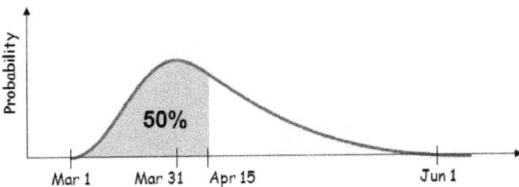

- **2.3) I Can Say No:**
  - "This request has to be rejected because this is a point out of scope, as you can read in the approved scope statement. This will be included in a next phase of the project."
  - "Your change request is very interesting, but it will cause non-acceptance by these users and duplicate maintenance cost."
  - "If we are late on this activity, that other on the seller's side will enter critical path, so any slippage on their delivery will impact our project schedule variance."
  - "Project could be finished 2 weeks before schedule, provided that Richard stays in the team full time for one more week."
  - "This change request has been analyzed: It would cause a secondary risk costing 2,000€ in mitigation and 2 weeks of delay. If response is not mitigation but containing, we need a reserve of 10,000€ and it will cost 3 weeks if it happened."

2.1) I Visualize Destiny and Path

Nowadays, many companies have teams assigned full time to project initiation. That is, before project approval, they analyze carefully if those projects are worth doing. They assess, for instance, if those project are profitable, opportunistic, aligned, affordable, etc.

While elaborating commercial bids, some companies manage them as real projects, with stakeholders named as bid managers, account managers, investment managers, etc.

Not long ago, I used to prepare many bids, often as much as three per week. Many of them were presented just for image. We already knew the client was not going to select us. Anyway, we had to submit a proposal of good quality. There was much *copy and paste*, of course, but we only got the feeling of a "good proposal" when we got something resembling a *draft version of a project plan.*

Clients will buy you a project because of the price, but also if they feel you have a clear vision about the final results and the way to get them. Therefore, you score high if you are able to communicate your understanding of requirements, scope and work packages. You get the entire client's attention when you explain how you are going to manage schedule, effort, risk, quality, communication, stakeholders and procurement.

You will get approval from your bosses if they feel you have a clear vision about cost, financing, needed resources (internal or coming from third parties), risks, acceptance criteria, legal liabilities, etc.

As you probably are noticing, the enumerated items above are the elements we should easily find in a typical project management plan. That's the reason why in the initiation phase it is good practice to have a Project Manager involved —if possible, an effective one with good planning skills. Let's claim to our organizations to have this good practice, but more importantly, let's apply those tools and techniques when we have the opportunity as Project Managers, when we are involved in a project not yet approved. We should never work without a realistic and complete plan, and it's never too early to start planning: We can make assumptions on what we don't know yet.

You need to put your imagination (that precious human gift) to work at full speed when you start managing a project. First thing first day, an Effective Project Manager has to start imagining the big picture. You rather have two pictures to imagine: 1) The product of the project or to-be scenario and 2) The roadmap to get there.

The powerful imagination of Effective Project Managers allows them to answer to questions like: *How will needs and goals change during the lifecycle of the project? How will be the roll out phase to move to production state? How will maintenance be operated? What features will the final product include and what not? How it will be used?* To get this vision it is very important the ability to break the whole into parts —but please don't fall into *paralysis by analysis* here.

Regarding the roadmap to get the to-be scenario, a very useful technique is to start visualizing the end as soon as possible: What should I deliver to get customer acceptation? And then visualize intermediate steps rewinding until today.

Some advice when using your crystal ball: 1) Write down, prepare documents and presentations: Imagination is reinforced by feedback loops coming when we write down or draw what we think. 2) Update your planning progressively as you discover new information. 3) Don't do this alone: Start delegating on team members by involving them in the planning process.

2.2) I Keep an Updated Credible Plan

When contracting a fixed price project, I've observed this step sequence many times:

1. A good proposal is made including many project planning elements like: activity schedule, milestone schedule, releases plan, resource effort plan, WBS, work descriptions, identified risks, communication plan, etc.

2. The client selects that seller. The seller wins the contract.

3. The contract is signed and kickoff meeting is held: overall purpose of following the initial plan, more or less, is heard.

4. Execution starts: The original plan is forgotten.

Conclusion: The initial plan was just a *selling artifact*. Nobody took it too seriously. Client admits not using it because there were a lot of inaccuracies given the seller team's logical ignorance over goals, constraints, and specific context not written in the RFP. Initial planning is only to be used if contract is not closed right, in order to negotiate or litigate.

I can see this flaw in above sequence: Between steps 2) and 3), since project is won until kickoff meeting, the seller and client teams should meet during several days in order to get an initial planning more real. Everybody understands contract legal bounds have to be supported by faithful planning agreed to parts. This seems to be responsible and also very productive work.

What comes next, keeping the plan updated, is more difficult.

With the help of planning tools, planning has to keep continually updated. Planning has to be used in each follow-up meeting to say: "This is what we had to do past week; this we have done and this is to be done next week."

In our profession there are many planning tools widespread used like Microsoft Project®, which for many Project Managers is a *de facto standard*[11]. There are many tools but, are we proficient at them? I know many Project Managers that just used Project® to draw *gantts*, but they don't know how to assign resources, track progress, report actual work, manage cost, etc. This was my own case until I took a serious training. Now that I use Project regularly I can say it saves me much time and I get a true feeling of anticipation and control, which I can easily communicate with *tracking gantt* figures like this:

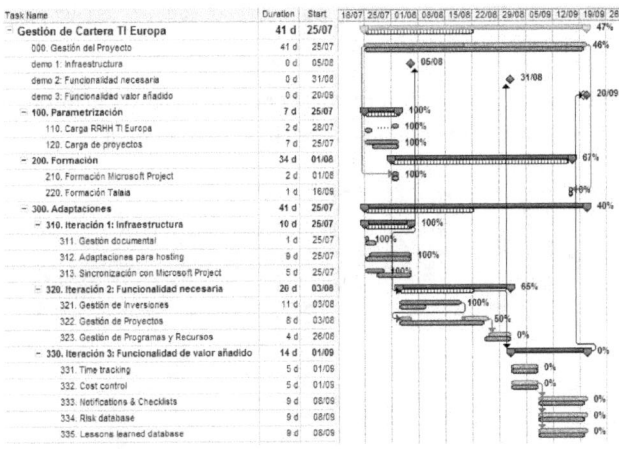

---

[11] A colleague told me once that the Project Managers at his company revealed when management threatened to get rid of Microsoft Project© licenses. I recall his indignation: "Removing Project to project managers is like removing Excel to accountants!"

Effective Project Managers are disciplined when using planning tools: They update new information as soon as they know —not needed tasks anymore, new tasks, new dates forecast, resource turnover, new needs on human or material resources, etc. The main benefit of using a planning tool this way is that with low effort they can prepare a status and performance report covering communication needs of stakeholders:

- To team members: When are they supposed to start and finish activities? What is the cumulated delay? What is the impact?
- To client and sponsor: Global and detailed progress per control account or activity. Up to date variances and forecasting on schedule and cost.
- To the PMO: Actual effort and cost and forecasting per group, per week, per month, quarter, year... Resource needs, leveling, EVM graphs, etc.

Other useful way to represent Project scope and progress is through a WBS with the percentage of completion on each control account:

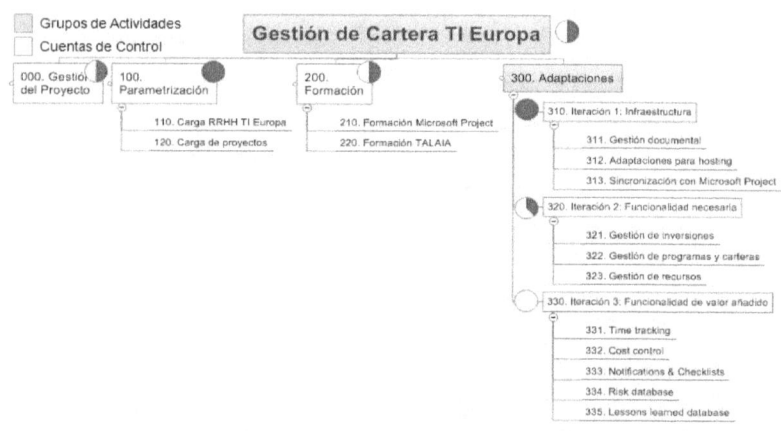

2.3) I Can Say No

As discussed in chapter 3, the nose is one essential body part of a Project Manager. I remember with great satisfaction how I could reject some offer to take over an irrecoverable project. I also regretfully remember other occasions I could not avoid to be appointed to project that I smelled as future failures.

In today corporations, when you say no to a project, you are taking much risk in your professional career. Some other times you cannot avoid to be in or out of a project because it's simply not your decision.

Once we are in, situation changes a bit. Now we are on the saddle. We are more on our control zone. We are supposed to have some kind of authority. Managing is taking decisions. To take effective decisions, a Project Manager has to have crystal clear what the project has to achieve (habit 2.1) and what are we achieving (habit 2.2). With the habit 2.3 we avoid not to achieve.

Saying "No!" to everything, without reasoning, is neither effective nor professional. It's quite the opposite to say "No!" because you have another burning "Yes!" inside. This burning "Yes!" in Project Management, is again an updated plan.

Each stakeholder should understand that if they request a change out of scope, affecting time and cost constraints, or impacting to other project goals, that request should be rejected. Conversely, change requests increasing project opportunities are well taken by Effective Project Managers.

The key to say No! (or Yes!) in an effective way, is to put first project interests, before personal interests. The best way to communicate and support these decisions is through a complete, updated credible plan.

4. The Habits of Effective Project Managers

4.3 Habit 3. Controlling the project

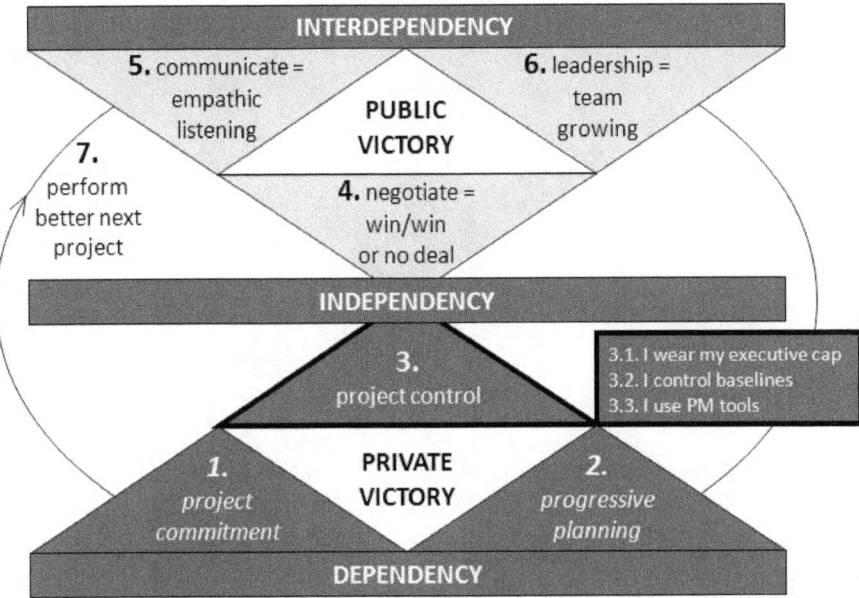

4. The Habits of Effective Project Managers

The 3rd Habit of Effective People: Put First Things First

The third habit of highly effective people, according to Covey is "put first things first". The first habit says "you are the programmer", the second says "you write the program", the third says "you run the program". The second habit addresses first creation, the mental creation, using imagination and conscience. The third habit addresses physical creation, using independent will. This is the habit of *getting things done*.

Effective people are used to getting what they mean. They usually apply discipline, pushing with big drive and effort. These people *walk the talk*. They don't necessarily like doing what they do, but their purpose is stronger than their disliking.

When we say a person outstands at effectiveness, this doesn't mean they do every task, or than they do much more tasks than the rest —don't confuse efficiency with effectiveness. These people have developed the habit of getting done the things they consider important overall, but not just sometimes, but regularly.

According to Covey, effective people usually work on not urgent but important tasks —see quadrant II of figure next page. Any task could be categorized as: urgent and important (quadrant I); not urgent but important (quadrant II); urgent but not important (quadrant III) and not urgent and not important (quadrant IV).

Tasks of quadrant I have to be done right now, they are needed. If you stay too much on quadrant I you get stressed and get the feeling of being reactive. Task of quadrant III should be delegated. If you work too much on quadrant III you get disappointed —these tasks maybe are important to others, not for you. Quadrant IV tasks should be avoided because they waste our precious time.

You can get a simple performance indicator of your effectiveness just measuring how long and how many tasks you close on quadrant II.

How can you move your balance to quadrant II? You need to anticipate, to plan your time. You are familiar with to-do-list, aren't you? You enumerate things ahead and you cross tasks out as you close them. When you get rid of the last item of the day gives you a feeling of achievement and personal satisfaction. This is our daily image of effective self-management.

	URGENT	NOT URGENT
IMPORTANT	• Crisis • Pressing problems • Deadline-driven projects, meetings, preparations necessity	• Preparation • Prevention • Values clarification • Planning • Relationship building • True re-creation • Empowerment effectiveness
NOT IMPORTANT	• Needless interruptions • Unnecessary reports • Unimportant meetings, phone calls, mail • Other people's minor issues deception	• Trivia busywork • Some phone calls • Time-wasters • "Escape" activities • Irrelevant mail • Excessive TV, Internet surfing, relaxation waste

Unfortunately, in this era of Information Society, for knowledge workers, a simple to-do-list is a valid tool no longer. The cause is mainly electronic mail. Nowadays is considered normal if you get between 100-200 daily emails, most of them relevant for your job. If this is the case, chances are your email inbox is your to-do-list properly. You feel stressed. The urgent outpaces the important. Your job consists of basically on putting out fires. You got down by a wave in the beach, you get up and another wave get you down again and again.

In this context effectiveness is possible. You should first schedule time for the task really important and not urgent (*big rocks*). Other quadrants' tasks will continue entering, but chances are you close a good number of *big rocks*. Conversely, if you deal with *big rocks* after other tasks, chances are you never start with them. Your email inbox with 100 new emails a day will always have another email to get into, won't it?

At this point, before continue, I'd like you to see a video by Stephen Covey called "*Big Rocks*"[12], that brilliantly illustrates the analogy between time management and the technique to fill a jar with big and little stones. What would you put first?

---

[12] Video is available at: http://goo.gl/5RgBL

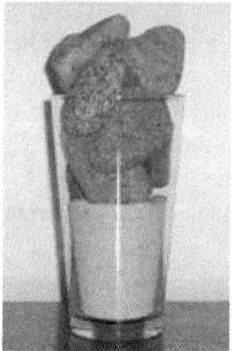

According to Covey, last generation personal planning tools should have these features:

- They must connect personal mission and values, personal roles as complete person, long term goals and day to day tasks.

- Long term goals should be structured throughout intermediate steps.

- Personal planning should be developed in the timeframe of a week. When planning an effective life, it is agreed that weeks are better management units than days. Common advice is to devote time once a week (on Friday afternoon? Sunday?) to design our weekly compass, by answering questions like: As a worker, father, spouse, friend, what is the important thing you have to do this week? What do you have to do to sharpen the saw —that is: to increase my long term production capacity? This way you can deduce your big rocks for the week.

▪ Then you have to schedule tasks or meetings to address, in the physical plane, goals and big rocks. For the whole set of pending tasks, it is important to prioritize according to importance level (vital -A-, important -B-, optional -C-) y assign a number according priority[13]. Some related activities could be grouped as a "project".

▪ Since most knowledge workers today use email client to manage their agenda, tasks and meetings, another important feature is that personal planning tool could be integrated with email client.

---

[13] For instance: B2 tasks have more priority than B4 or C1, but less priority than A4.

The 3rd Habit of Effective Project Managers:
Project Control

Effective Project Managers are supposed to be good at time management. We don't want leading a project a person who doesn't even have time to respond to emails, or is always busy with trivial non important things. Regarding Project Managers, third habit goes beyond that. It's not enough that Project Manager is well organized on the personal level. The Project Manager is representing the project in front of stakeholders. His personal objectives match the project goals. We consider him effective in time management only if the project is progressing at the desired pace. That's maybe the main reason because he is at charge: *to control the project timing*. We need someone taking care of deadlines, costs and deliverables. Many people consider a Project Manager is effective if he can get things done on time and on budget. An Effective Project Manager has *to master project controlling*.

With the second habit, Effective Project Managers organize in their mind what has to be done. With the third habit, they try to do what has been promised. This habit has to do very much with *hard skills*. We are lucky to have many tools and techniques that probed to be effective. There is plenty of formal and informal training on hard skills for a Project Manager.

Unfortunately for Project Managers not proficient on project control, evidences speak for themselves. We are mercilessly criticized by everybody. It's like a plumber fixing a pipe incorrectly: *everyone can see the leaks*.

Imagine you are a Project Sponsor. You enter the elevator and bump into your Project Manager:

–Sponsor: Good to see you! How is my project going?

–Project Manager: Oh, well... so and so. We'll be missing Mike. He happens to leave the company and the team is going to suffer his lost...

–Sponsor: Mike? Who the heck is Mike?

–Project Manager: He's our data base administrator, I guessed you knew him. This is bad! I don't know what we are going to do without him...

–Sponsor: So... Do I have to tell the client we're delivering late?

–Project Manager: That could be fine, yes.

–Sponsor: How long? What corrective actions are we taking? How much is it going to cost us? Why didn't we have a backup?

–Project Manager: To be honest, Mike departure is not a big deal. The big problem it's just we cannot cope with all these new issues: day after day they are still changing requirements!

–Sponsor: No, this cannot be! We cannot say yes to everything. This is a fixed price contract. I'll go and see him tomorrow. Please give me the change log, the risk register and the estimate to complete.

–Project Manager: Hmm... good... I get off this floor. Later on I will send you an email...

As you know, you will not get any email this afternoon, neither this evening, nor tomorrow morning. He will give you the perfect excuse: there were other urgent issues to attend. What is your impression when you think of him? Do you see him like an effective Project Manager? What if HR asks your opinion for his annual performance appraisal?

Even worse: What would have thought the CEO if he or she were in the same elevator, at the same time, listening to the conversation right there? Just talking to a Project Manager at the elevator you can get a sense of his effectiveness. Now let's rewind the scene a bit. You enter the same elevator again, but this time you meet an Effective Project Manager:

–Sponsor: Good to see you! How is my project going?

–Effective Project Manager: I need you to see your email inbox. That risk identified two weeks ago has just occurred. I need your approval to recruit another data base administrator from the selected seller. You recall we had approved a two month subcontracting for 10,000 €. This cost overrun will reduce project margin only by half a point.

–Sponsor: Affecting the deadline?

–Effective Project Manager: Provided that I have him next Monday, as they ensure, there will be no slippage for this reason…

–Sponsor: For this reason? Are you worried for another thing?

–Effective Project Manager: It's just the rework level we are supporting. This week they have changed specifications by the third time. I can estimate we have produced 500 function points just to be thrown away. This costs another 10,000 € !!

–Sponsor: So, what do you suggest?

–Effective Project Manager: I've prepared three alternatives to reduce scope. There is a PowerPoint presentation attached in my email. Do you have time now? I'd like to present this to you. I think we should go tomorrow to see the client…

Can you see the difference? This Project Manager is giving an image of effectiveness. What is his secret?

Mainly, I would say his secret is quantitative control. Each time, he i sable to measure the gap between what *is* happening and what *should be* happening —we use the term *baseline* for this. He can adapt communication to stakeholders for they are not supposed to be familiar with the jargon.

The third habit of highly effective people "put first things first" could be translated as the generic habit of 3) Project Control and other three specific sub-habits: 3.1) I Wear my Executive Cap; 3.2) I Control Baselines and 3.3) I Use Project Management Tools :

- 3.1) I Wear my Executive Cap: You can act like the CEO of a small company. You can delegate effectively. You can communicate performance with a business oriented language. You log significant facts just in case you need this information afterwards.

- 3.2) I Control Baselines: You proactively manage variances proposing preventive and corrective actions —you plan and control them as well. You perform scope change management. You are accountable for getting things done. You take the authority even when you are not officially empowered.

- 3.3) I Use Project Management Tools: Quantitative analysis is not easily improvised. When we are asked a punctual explanation on schedule variances, for instance, we can improvise an Excel spreadsheet or a PowerPoint presentation. The problem arises if we need to do that every week. Then we won't have time to other things. We won't manage the project effectively. Nowadays there are many good tools to support Project Manager's job. If properly used, then quantitative analysis is effortless.

3.1) I Wear my Executive Cap

Somewhere I read that a Project Manager should think and act like a CEO of a small company, being that enterprise the project itself. How should you behave when appointed as a CEO at MYPROJECT Inc.? If you have the habit of committing, then you will feel responsible of effectively managing resources (money, people, materials, etc.) entrusted to you. If you have the habit of planning, you will know better than anyone about the vision, mission, values, short and long term objectives, potential threats and opportunities, relationships with third parties, process assets, quality standards, etc.

Those two habits (committing and planning) are really important, but for a CEO, it may be more important the habit of "getting things done":

- CEOs don't do the work themselves, they **delegate effectively** on stewardships —they don't treat people like "gofers" as if they didn't have any judgment. It is not very effective directing on each task, nor going deep inside into details. Any effective delegation implies agreeing on five areas: 1) the desirable results; 2) the guidelines on how to do; 3) the available resources; 4) the evaluation mechanisms and 5) the consequences of good and bad performance.

- However, delegates don't do everything. CEOs devote most of their time to **executive communication**. Reporting about getting things done and results does not have to saturate with operation details. As the CEO of MYPROJECT Inc., when you speak in the "shareholders' meeting", your messages have to be clear, synthetic, information based, factual. You summarize what has happened in the past and predict what is going to happen in the near future. Steering committee members ask high level questions that you had already anticipated. Your answers are straight to the point.

- And last, but not least, the ugliest part of being a CEO is that **mistakes are paid**: you can be accused, demoted, destitute, even prosecuted! Some mistakes are yours, some are from others. To protect yourself from other's mistakes, the only thing you can do is what I call "expiation management". Maybe it is not necessary in the end, but it doesn't do any harm if you maintain a log with the significant events, decisions taken, who did what when, who originated the issues, who assumed what risks, what was the own judgment and advice, etc.

In our field of Project Management, there are many well known techniques to produce an **"executive communication"**. Here we are just three examples:

- Communicating on cost and schedule variations could be based on the standard **EVM** (Earned Value Management).
- Scope control can be graphically expressed on a **WBS** diagram, with the percentage of completion on control accounts.
- Status reports could be institutionalized across the organization. Receivers would appreciate the use of **dashboards** and **RAG** indicators —Red: the project is now off-plan and drastic action is needed; Amber: substantial or corrective action is required; Green: the project is on-track and likely to meet expectations.

Regarding **"expiation management"**, I'd like to give just two recommendations for starters: 1) a risk register and 2) a project log.

3.2) I Control Baselines

The habit of *getting things done*, in Project Management, has much to do with *getting the plan done*. Although project plan is a live document constantly changing, we must never forget the initial approved plan. There are many project plan elements we are not able to measure quantitatively, but on those other measurable elements, our responsibility is to measure the gap between what *is* happening and what *should be* happening. In our profession, what *should be* happening is called *baseline*.

According to PMBOK®, every Project has three baselines: scope baseline (*Are we doing what we are supposed to deliver?*); schedule baseline (*Are we on time, late, early?*) and cost performance baseline (*Are we on cost, with cost overrun, under cost?*)

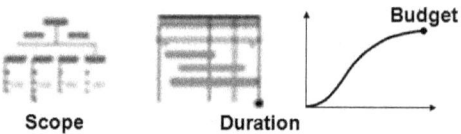

Scope   Duration   Budget

To measure scope, you can indicate percentage of completion on control account nodes of the WBS (*Work Breakdown Structure*). If you want to measure schedule, you can represent percentage of completion for each activity and compare planned versus actual start and finish dates. If you want to measure cost performance, you can compare earned cost of work performed versus actual cost of work performed and planned cost of work scheduled.

As you can see, there are many already invented ways for measuring baselines, but measuring and controlling are different things. Control means limiting the distance between what it is and what should be.

PMBOK® advises us to apply corrective and preventive actions, defect repairing, change management, etc. Let's use these terms to name what we need to keep registered, but it maybe is more important what we don't register in documents because we don't have time —or we don't need to register.

You can get things done, or control baselines, if you take initiative. There are things falling inside our control zone, the rest are in our concern zone:

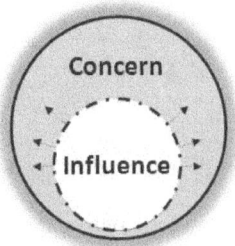

According to Covey, there are 7 degrees of initiative that you could take proactively. The more initiative, the more autonomy and control:

1. I wait for instructions
2. I ask
3. I recommend
4. I ask for permission
5. I do and report immediately
6. I do and report periodically
7. I do

Over the things not in your control zone:

1. You could wait for instructions over things not directly of your competence.
2. You could ask questions over those parts of your job you don't know how to decide.
3. You could recommend a solution so that person in charge decide easily —but the decision will be his not yours.

On initiative level 4) ask for permission, you get more power than 3) recommend a solution, in the sense that is your decision, not other's. On initiative levels 5-7, you take the initiative at doing your job inside your control zone, reporting more or less as your autonomy level requires.

In my opinion, the frontier between control and concern zones is not clearly defined for a Project Manager. An Effective Project Manager doesn't want to wait for instructions, ask or recommend solutions. In an uncertainty environment (like every project is) you don't get things done right this way.

Effective Project Managers should take initiative levels 5-7 not just for things inside their control zone, but for the things on their concern zone. The ongoing effect is that, little by little, their control circle widens. We must consider that stakeholders, on the project sake, generally encourages and tolerate those limits are questioned and overtaken by project managers.

When a Project Manager decides, on his own, to do something or take a decision related to the project, stakeholders are hardly upset because he is exceeding his competence level. They prefer a project manager taking initiative.

Quite often, *Effective Project Managers prefer to apologize after than ask for permission first.*

> *Effective Project Managers often prefer to apologize after than ask for permission first*

The most inspirational text I've ever read about the attitude of taking initiative in uncertainty environments, to get things done, is "A Message To Garcia".

"A Message To Garcia" was a short text written by Elbert Hubbard in 1899, noticing that the real hero of the Cuba War was Rowan, the American official who carried a letter to general Calixto Garcia from president McKiley with instructions to arrange the insurgence. General Garcia was hidden in the heart of the Cuba jungle.

When Rowan was commissioned, he did not ask "Where is he at?"

He took the letter, sealed it up in an oilskin pouch, strapped it over his heart, in four days landed by night off the coast of Cuba from an open boat, disappeared into the jungle, and in three weeks came out on the other side of the Island, having traversed a hostile country on foot, and delivered his letter to Garcia.

The expression *to carry a Message to Garcia* became a common one in American jargon. It means *taking initiative*. Many people keep using that expression without knowing about its origin[14].

We want to be like Rowan !!!

---

[14] A Message to Garcia was one of the first best sellers in history. There were edited over 40 million copies, being translated into 37 languages. It was adapted to two cinema movies and there was also a radio adaptation. You can read the original text at: http://goo.gl/I9S2g

3.3) I Use Project Management Tools

Unfortunately, many good Project Managers, who has good experience, project management fundamentals and good professionals on their teams, encounter the problem that do not have good tools to seamlessly use their knowledge. For them, passing the PMP® exam is *like getting a driver's license and then realizing they can only walk*. Sometimes, even worse, the performing organization requires them *to go by bus*, by imposing tools overloading them with huge bureaucracy. Project Managers need to manage a project, not a tool. Especially, they need to manage expectations of all stakeholders, with an effective and efficient communication, providing information in the right format, at the right time, with the appropriate impact and only the necessary information. As regards their personal self-management and team management, they need to manage documentation, communication, changes, deliverables, schedule, cost, risks, issues, procurement, calendars, team members' performance, etc.

Good tools can support some project management knowledge areas. This is quite remarkable especially for cost and schedule management. There is a great difference on productivity between a Project Manager using Excel® to represent schedule and other using Project®. Difference is bigger when they need to monitor and control costs. Imagine that you have your team members' timesheets and expense sheets and progress reported on each activity. You prepare a weekly cost performance report —including variances and forecasting. If you use Excel® to elaborate that report every week, would you have time to manage the project? Multiply the effort needed for 20 Project Managers sharing the same problem. Would your company need to hire an expensive PMO team just for this?

There is a great range of project management tools to get this automated (be them proprietary or open source, licensed or SaaS). Select the best tool for you and your organization, and more importantly: *have the good habit of using it well.*

4. The Habits of Effective Project Managers

4.4 Habit 4. Negotiating (Win-Win or No Deal)

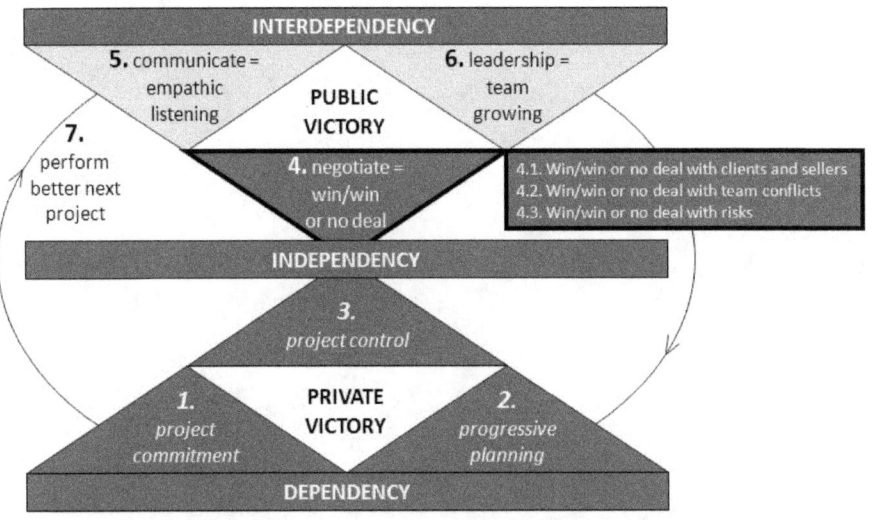

Separate the people from the problem
Focus on interests not positions
Invent options for mutual gain
Insist on using objective criteria

ROGER FISHER, WILLIAM URY: Getting to YES!

4. The Habits of Effective Project Managers

The Three Habits for Public Victory

When a Project Manager has integrated on his character the first three habits, we can say of him that he is effective on a private level. He has confidence as a Project Manager. He is proficient at hard skills. However, private victories are insufficient for project success. A Project Manager can be highly proactive and get totally identified with project goals (habit 1. Project Commitment). He can continually visualize next steps and anticipate problems (habit 2. Progressive Planning). He can also exerts tight control to minimize variances (habit 3. Project Control). He can do all that and fail as a Project Manager.

I know the case of a Project Manager who led a team of 10 highly proficient experts during 12 months in a software development project abroad:

- The product of the project was scored high technically but perceived as poor quality by client.
- The relationship with the prime contractor (who had business interests contradictory with project success) was not good at all.
- The economic result was as bad as a net loss of 170,000€.

This project, quite promising at the beginning, ended up as an awful experience, especially for that Project Manager, who despite doing his best at the personal level, was not able to get a public victory.

A Project Manager can be effective at the personal level (he can make and keep promises) but the project could be a failure. Why would that happen?

- Firstly, the Project is not done by the Project Manager, team members do. The Project Manager *conducts the orchestra*, no less. However, no matter how good the Project Manager, the project will probably be finished late, with cost overrun and poor quality if team members are burnt out, or they don't get along at work, or they are not technically prepared, for instance. If his staff isn't up to the job at hand, the project will fail.

- Secondly, the project affects to a stakeholder community unpredictable, out of reach and control. There are generally lots variables out of the control zone of the Project Manager: stakeholders, environmental factors, interrelationships, uncertainties, unforeseen issues, constraints, etc.

Most projects are prone to uncertainty and risk. Tom DeMarco said: "If a project has no risks, don't do it."[15] To make things worse, throughout project lifecycle, there are always continuous changes in scope[16].

Projects can be closed only when stakeholders meet of exceeds their expectations. In other words, projects end when stakeholders are happy. Could it be a finish goal more ambiguous, imprecise and undetermined than that?

---

[15] Waltzing with Bears: Managing Risk on Software Projects. Tom DeMarco & Timothy Lister, Ed. Dorset House Publishing, 2003.

[16] One technique to protect against scope creep is an integrated change management system.

The kind of control a Project Manager could aspire is of the kind *stochastic* but *deterministic*. You have a *deterministic* control, for instance over the gas pressure on a vessel. If you control temperature and volume variables, then you can control absolutely gas pressure. You have *stochastic* control over the rate at which employees leave your company to take jobs with the competition. Variables like salary and benefits and work hours and pressure have a tendency to affect the leave-rate, but no matter how correctly you set them, there is no guarantee that John will stay till the project ends.

In the Project Management field, if you have a capable team working with synergy, if you manage client expectations right, if you have good communication with the sponsor, the steering committee and the rest of stakeholders, if you have enough time and resources, then the project will *probably* be a success but nobody can guarantee you that. There is not any recipe, tool, technique, practice granting that project goals are met.

As discussed earlier, Project Managers should widen their control zone beyond the limits of authority they are granted. To be successful on the interdependent reality of a project, you must transform your concerning zone into your influence zone. Most stakeholders see this as proactivity and Project Manager's initiative. Authority limits in Project Management are not usually clearly established.

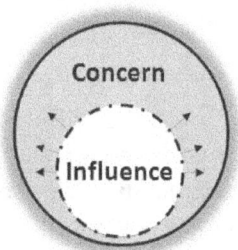

This attitude of crossing borders, of being comfortable with uncertainty and changes, makes us to look out for help: We are not alone in Project Management.

In order to get public victories, you have to *involve people in the problem and seek the solution with them.*

> *To get public victories, you have to involve People in the problem and seek the Solution with them*

In this sense, an Effective Project Manager has to be:

- A Good Negotiator
- A Good Communicator
- A Good Leader

Many people think these three attributes are innate, especially leadership (*a good leader is born, not made*). I argue that any Project Manager can incorporate these attributes on his character, sooner or later, if he toils practicing these three habits of public victory:

- <u>Habit 4) Negotiate = Win-Win or No Deal</u>: The habit of negotiation base don principles.
- <u>Habit 5) Communicate = Empathic Listening</u>: The habit of effective communication and stakeholder expectation management.
- <u>Habit 6) Leadership = Team Growing</u>: The habit of situational leadership.

The 4th Habit of Effective People: Think Win-Win

The fourth habit of highly effective people, according to Covey is "think win-win", or "win-win or no deal". You achieve public victories regularly only if you respect other's interests but at the same time you have courage and determination to defend your own interests as well. When there is a conflict, effective people don't think about winning at the expense of others.

Rather the opposite, they have the habit of getting to work with the other party to seek a solution (*every problem has a solution*) which makes everybody win. If win-win is not possible, if they only agree they don't agree, they prefer to stop negotiating before damaging the good relationship.

Life is full of conflicts. Conflicts appear because two parties' interest are incompatible. When facing a conflict we try to think with "scarcity paradigm". What one opponent wins the other loses: "If you see your favorite TV show, then I cannot see mine." "If we spend Christmas at your parents', then we'll spend New Year with mine's." "If you hire a new resource, then you'll have to dismiss Mike."

Effective people know that problems don't get solved so easily. Quick win-lose solutions don't last very much. Covey said: "With people, slow is fast, and fast is slow." Effective people use to confront problems with the "abundance paradigm" in mind. In this Information Society we just have partial information most of the time. There is always a better solution than two parts would get on their side.

Effective and lasting solutions can only be found working together, on the same side of the table, the problem ahead.

Moreover, in the process you build true relationships. Two people getting a win-win solution together create solid bounds. Effective people don't fear conflict. Conversely, they see conflicts as opportunities for public victories.

The 4th Habit of Effective Project Managers: Negotiate = Win-Win or No Deal

If you manage projects, then you are used to negotiating and conflict solving. Many projects start sinking at the very moment a good agreement is not made, or when a conflict is poorly solved. The name for this fourth habit is the same for effective people and for Effective Project Managers, but there is a big difference: *It's not the Project Manager the one who wins. The project wins.*

To get practice with this fourth habit, the Project Manager has to leave his ego aside and get identified with project goals. Only this way he could take effective decisions, very tough sometimes, as for instance: advice early closing to the sponsor, dismiss a team worker, communicate to the steering committee that critical deadline is going to be missed, etc.

As Project Managers, we lose effectiveness when we defend our position in an egocentric way.

When managing projects, egocentric identification with the project is not advisable because get you thinking in terms of scarcity:

- "Client has rejected this delivery. He finally told me this functionality was not necessary. This makes throw two workweeks away!"
- "Since the expert I was requiring has been assigned to other project, I hope the steering committee doesn't get too surprised if I finish late."
- "If they want me I finish earlier, I'll have to reduce scope or quality."

Better to criticize people, or focus on people positions, an Effective Project Manager should focus on project's interest and invent options for mutual gain.

- *Client has rejected this delivery because functionality was not necessary.* Obviously this seems to produce a serious impact for the project, but before assuming the loss, you have to investigate the cause and propose corrective or preventive actions. This functionality could be proposed in future phases or future projects? Do we have to improve requirement management and testing processes? Do we need to request an increase on budget or schedule, or a scope reduction to meet project goals?
- *I don't have the expert I need*: It doesn't mean there is not another valid expert available, in or outsourced. Could I try to negotiate a temporary assignation with the resource responsible?
- *Project duration has been shortened:* This makes new risks appear: go and manage them! Nobody obliges you to deliver a poor quality product to client.

The important thing to remember is that *Project Manager is never alone.* He is not the only stakeholder. Projects are developed in an interdependent environment.

> *You have to involve people in the problem and seek the solution with them*

Any time you have **to manage a conflict or a negotiation**, you have to confront the situation with a positive and optimistic spirit of **"abundance paradigm"**. If an agreement beneficial to the project is not possible, then you can agree on always available option of **"No Deal"**.

The fourth habit of highly effective people "think win-win" could be translated this way to the field of Project Management:

- **4.1) Win-Win or No Deal with Clients and Sellers**: Los **clients and final users** of the project's product, cause conflicts when they reject changes in the new way of doing things after the project, or whey they are not happy with the results, etc. These conflicts are the same in nature as when Project Manager is the client of a **seller** who is providing a project part in procurement.

- **4.2) Win-Win or No Deal with Team Conflicts**: Many times, the worst conflicts are "cooked" inside the **team**. Remember a project can fail simply because *two team members don't get along.*

- **4.3) Win-Win or No Deal Managing Risks**: An Effective Project Manager look for the colective benefit when managing **uncertainty** be them in the form of threats or opportunities.

4.1) Win-Win or No Deal with Clients and Sellers

One afternoon I got a call from Manuel, a colleague. Manuel was a senior Project Manager, with a lot of experience. He was working with us not a long time, but he had accumulated a large background managing projects before. The reason of his call was precise and clear: *He wanted to know the best way to communicate a client we stopped providing our services.* The contract had a clause allowing us to do that on the ground of non-fulfillment on payments. So, Manuel had decided to get the three team members back. I stopped what I was doing and went to his office to talk with him. This was, more or less, the conversation we held:

–Jose: What's the problem?

–Manuel: Look at this email from Luis, the client. He's telling me he's not paying the last two bills because the software development processes we have defined are not useful if not implemented with software lifecycle management tools. Now he's asking for tools!

–Jose: The RFP did not required tooling, did it?

–Manuel: The problem is that Luis just *doesn't know what he need*. He's appointed accountable of gaining CMMI certification this year, but technical people in IT department are always coping with urgent demands from the business, not following any process. He asked for these 18 processes written down and published on the intranet and so we did. Now somebody has convinced him that technical people are keen for tools, and just by using tools they are going to work better and faster. That's nonsense!

–Jose: You don't think imposing tools make them get CMMI certified more easily…

–Manuel: That's the other way around, Jose! It will take longer! In June, the lead appraiser will perform the first audit. When he checks people don't understand processes, but use tools blindly instead, the non-conformance list will be so extensive that certification will come one year later, at best.

–Jose: Luis will not understand that imposing tools is against project goals?

–Manuel: I don't think so. He's not familiar with the problem. This project is quite a challenge for him. Besides, he has no authority on technical people. In this context is utterly impossible for them to get certified. Our team has low morale. If he says he's not paying, we can oblige him by contract. He get the project canceled but it's not his fault. We get paid what they owe and we can relocate our team into other projects. Everybody wins.

–Jose: Are you sure everybody wins? Have you talked with our legal department? Do you want to start litigating because he owes two bills?

–Manuel: Well, I don't think it will happen... But in that case, law is in on our side, isn't it? I'm about to send him this email. It took me the whole afternoon. Tell me what you think about it...

I read the email out loud, while I was noticing how changed his expression: 1) pride; 2) doubt; 3) regret and finally 4) shame.

When you react by email something curious happens. You have a lot of reasons in your head. You start writing and structuring them here and there, ordering your arguments quite sophisticatedly. This is an addictive process. Your anger gets instant feedback as you read what you are written so reasonable and so eloquent. You imagine the effect on receivers (those in Cc and those in Bcc). You strive to write all they need to know, but taking care that they don't misunderstand against us. You write to be read by a fictitious tribunal that only exists in your mind.

.

You can take easily two, three hours, the whole afternoon, writing in flux, without noticing the passing time. You write, you read, you get aware how right you are, you get angrier, than so it goes the negative spiral. I've lived this experience many times. How many times I've thought "I better send it tomorrow", just to check next morning the stupidity I was about to send?

It didn't take me too long to convince Manuel the best thing he could do was to go and see Luis as soon as possible. The best option for Manuel was not to litigate. In litigations neither side wins, everybody loses. Legal fees are only part of the cost; the litigants may end up using as much or more manpower on the litigation as was expended on the entire contract under dispute. Litigations drag on forever, often longer than the term of the original contract. In general, litigations, as wars, are agreements of the kind lose-lose.

Mi colleague Manuel was to talk with his client Luis, not to defend his position:

> "The processes are documented and delivered on due date. If you don't pay me I cancel the project."

Neither was he to talk to Luis to attack his position:

> "Tools don't get more quality by themselves. Processes and people are more important than tools for change management projects."

Manuel followed my advice and was there with a constructive spirit. *We see the world not as it is, but as we are.* Manuel had prejudices against software lifecycle management tools. Luis had prejudices against *theoretical processes that don't get practical use.* Each of them knew his slice of truth, as good or bad, as respectful.

First thing Manuel had to do was to ask these to questions to Luis:

- "Can we go for a solution that is better than mine or yours?"

- "For me it's very important that we maintain our good relationship. If we don't get a mutual beneficial agreement, would you mind if we conclude "No Deal", so that we escalate the problem to our hierarchy?"

Luis answered yes to both questions and they arranged a meeting.

Second step was to define the problem. Instead of justifying his position, Manuel told Luis:

- "It seems we have different opinions regarding the approach to this project. I need to listen to you. Please explain me your point with all details."

After listening the explanations of Luis, Manuel summarized with his own words. Luis corrected some points, but in the end he felt understood.

Then, Manuel asked:

- "Now. Would you be willing to listen to me the way I listened to you?"

Of course, Luis listened patiently to Manuel explanations giving all his attention. Once clear and understood each point of view, they started working together to propose solutions, not as opponents but partners on the same side of the table, with the problem ahead, seeking the best for the project goals. Among other options they considered, they finally decided a new approach, *a third alternative*, they never would have discovered on their own:

> "Continuous training on CMMI processes to technical people, implementing an agile software process using tools for monitoring and dashboard reporting on tests, defects, amount and importance of remaining tasks."

My first recommendation with there is a conflict with a client is confronting as soon as possible. These kinds of problems are rarely solved with time. We Project Managers have the responsibility of acting.

Projects are prone to disagreements and mutually incompatible interests, but in general, negotiation is easy than in other fields. If project is well founded (that is, due work is done in the initiation phase), then project goals are generally clear and agreed. Project Manager can recall initial decisions to propose clear criteria based on the best interest for the project. Projects are born so that everybody wins.

Project Manager has more information, but he doesn't know everything. When negotiating with clients and sellers, Project Manager's effectiveness relies on getting effective win-win agreements.

When you have managed quite projects, you get used to conflicts with clients and sellers. Moreover, you want these conflicts happen because you know that to-be scenario is better for project success and relationship between the parts. Conflicts are very interesting, but please you don't provoke them!

4. The Habits of Effective Project Managers

4.2) Win-Win or No Deal with Team Conflicts

In Project Management there are not many certain facts, but one every experience Project Manager agree on is this: *projects are prone to conflicts.* A conflict occurs when interests of two or more people are incompatible. Projects have plenty of incompatible interest and stakeholders. On the other side, team members, those knowledge workers responsible for activities being performed and products made with good quality, are keen to argue. Please pay attention, this is important: People having arguments are not sign of bad performance. Good professionals are argumentative. They like their jobs and defend their positions and decisions. The more professionals they are, the more arguments they have. An Effective Project Manager should worry when there are no arguments in the team, especially in the initial phases. If that is the case, he should wonder: Are team members giving 100% of potential? Are they collaborating with each other? Are they motivated and truly committed?

> *Good professionals are argumentative: The more professionals they are, the more arguments they have*

Team members expect a lot of the Project Manager. The least a Project Manager can do for them is to get rid of the external noise distracting the team from real work like client's or hierarchy's pressures, politics, etc. Other basic need the Project Manager should provide is everything regarding the working conditions for optimal performance —team room, tools, documentation, etc.

This is easy. The difficult part to provide has to do with the psychological conditions of team working. The Project Manager should invest many funds in the *emotional bank account* of each team member.

128 | The Habits of Effective Project Managers

You have to listen to them empathically until they feel totally understood. You have to attend to the little things, keep commitments, clarify expectations, show personal integrity, etc. The **Emotional Bank Account** paradigm proposed by Covey, is an excellent way to visualize the trusting level on the Project Manager. Effective Project Managers should measure, metaphorically speaking, emotional deposits and withdraws on team members. You make deposits on their emotional bank account when you give time to them, listen to them, do something for them, etc. You make withdraws when you ask them to do something for us without providing any explanation, when they want to talk but you have no time for them, when you ask an extra effort, etc. It's very important for you to know if you are in red numbers with some person: you cannot do more withdraws. Unlike normal bank accounts, to reconcile an emotional bank account you have to do small deposits continually.

> *How is my emotional bank account with Mike? Can I make a withdrawal right now? Should I make a deposit?*

If you have made enough deposits on team members, when a conflict arises between them, one of those conflicts threatening project goals, then you are in good position to solve the problem with them in an effective way. Effective solutions to project conflicts are not forced, nor smoothed. They rarely are solved with time. It's the responsibility of the Project Manager to confront the conflicts as soon as possible, and not closing a conflict until each part feels they have won with the solution.

Let's imagine this case: Mike and John have a conflict. They do their best to find a solution. When you know about the solution, you think that Mike wins and John loses. Then you should call Mike and John and tell them: "This solution doesn't look fine to me because Mike is winning and John is losing. I'm sure there has to be another solution that makes you both win. For the sake of the project, we should find a better alternative".

There is no silver bullet to find that kind of agreements "Win-win or No Deal" among team members, but there is some help.

For instance, in the bestselling book *Getting to YES!* [17] there is much good advice to avoid the positional way of managing conflicts, and to enhance the possibilities of a negotiation based on principles —always better for the project:

- **Separate the People from the Problem**: Be soft on the people, hard on the problem. Proceed independently of trust.
- **Focus on Interests Not Positions**: Explore interests. Avoid having a bottom line.
- **Invent Options for Mutual Gain**: Develop multiple options to choose from; decide later.
- **Insist on Using Objective Criteria**: Try to reach a result based on standards independent of will. Reason and be open to reason; yield to principle, not pressure.

---

[17] Getting to YES! Negotiating Agreement Without Giving In, Roger Fisher and William L. Ury, Ed. Penguin Group, 1981.

4.3) Win-Win or No Deal Managing Risks

Risks are inherent to projects. As Tom DeMarco said: "If a project has no risks, don't do it. You can manage projects by managing their risks." Effective risk management is worth doing for any stakeholder having much to lose or win with the project: the more uncertain the more worth managing. Include in the list of risk concerned stakeholders not only Project Managers, but sponsors, clients, performing organizations, etc. Effective Project Managers are certain their project will have expected and unexpected problems, issues and opportunities. They want problems, but they don't have crisis. The opposite of risk management is crisis management, trying to figure out what to do about the problem after it happens.

> *The opposite of Risk Management is Crisis Management*

Effective Project Managers are not afraid of risk. Conversely, they try to see risks as opportunities —even when they look like threats.

A company I used to work had what they called the Risk Management Steering Committee (RMSC). This group was formed by the most senior, largely experienced, gray haired, top managers in the company. When they met, they basically monitored and controlled risks of projects above a budget threshold. When my colleagues Project Managers had to go to RMSC meetings, they usually complained having to pass that additional control. They saw that as a nuisance: more reports to produce for more stakeholders —and they had much power in the company. Sometimes lamented: "If this project had been sold for 5000 € less, then I could avoid RMSC. Bad luck!" I told them they should think the other way around: "You are lucky. In the RMSC table there is money waiting for you!"

> *Wherever people meet to manage Risks: There is Money!*

As everybody knows, *managing risks cost money*. There are four typical responses to a negative risk:

- You can **mitigate** it: You take steps before its materialization to reduce eventual containment costs. These are the steps required in advance so that the containment strategy you've chosen will be implementable at transition time.

- You can **contain** it: You set aside sufficient time and money to pay for it, should it materialize. In practice, it doesn't make much sense to contain a single risk; instead, you contain your entire set of risks. Some of them will materialize and others won't. A containment strategy sets aside enough resources, on average, to offset the risks that are likely to materialize.

- You can **avoid** it: You don't do the project or the part of the project that entails the risk. The natural consequence of avoiding a risk is that you forgo the benefit that going into the risky area offered.

- You can **accept** it: You do none of the above and the risk just happens not to come back and bite you. It doesn't materialize. When you plan to evade a risk, you just cross fingers. This is the only response that cost no money, but if the problem does materialize, the impact is will cost you more money than you could have imagined.

When I was the one to go to RMSC, I thought: 1) In the RMSC table there is money waiting for me and 2) I can manage expiation. For me this was a pure win-win approach: Stakeholders won minimizing possible negative impacts; the project won increasing budget; I won passing blame.

Wherever People Meet to Manage Risks: There is Money!

My preparation for the RMSC meeting was like this: I selected the more important risks from the risk register. I produced a short presentation to provide high level information, using a business language, adapting my communication to RMSC members. Then I produced a quantitative analysis for the critical few, that is, I estimated they money impact should they occur, trying to justify well my basis of estimates. Finally, I proposed several alternative responses with cost details.

My goal was mainly to make their decision easier: "If this risk occurs, the impact cost for penalties and rework, weighted by probability is about 115,000€ and will cause a slippage of 5 weeks. If we could apply this mitigation response, costing only 10,000€, we will reduce probability of occurrence and our risk exposition will be 15,000€. Should we accept or mitigate?"

When they approved mitigation budget of 10,000€ they were aware that money will be lost if the risk didn't materialize. As I mentioned earlier, these people had a lot of experience. For them it was normal that risk management costs money. You didn't need to convince them on that. However, you had to offer a good detailed explanation on the basis of your estimates, which they even make bigger sometimes. In this committee I never heard any unconscious comment of the kind: "We are accepting this risk. Let's cross fingers to save good money! Make me accountable of this decision."

On my way to the RMSC meeting, I was feeling like a *stock market shark*. Sometimes I returned with more money and sometimes they made me see that my fears were unfounded. Very rarely the result was *to do more with less*. Almost always, the project won. No meetings more productive!

Managing Expiation at Risk Management Steering Committees

Many projects fail because, all of a sudden, it appears an unexpected problem that makes the project worthless. Risks are identified, a risk register is published, risks are reported on status reports, and mitigation strategies are approved. Risks are monitored and controlled. If one only reviews the risk lists and records, it appears that the project is low-risk. All the risks enumerated are at the inconvenience or nuisance level. The risk tracking proceeds without variance until the project is suddenly canceled. Those risks truly important were simply ignored. In words by Tom DeMarco: "People take elaborate care not to trip over the railroad ties, but nobody can see the oncoming train!"

> *People take elaborate care not to trip over the railroad ties, but nobody can see the oncoming train!*

Some examples of risks management ignoring *the oncoming train*:

- A consulting project to aid business development of SMEs in Egypt was canceled on March 2011. Nobody listed the risk of Hosni Mubarak's fall.

- One of our software development projects abroad was a financial failure because the prime contractor made us appear as responsible of functional flaws, when our team always understood we were responsible on the technical non functional part of the scope.

- Other example far to my experience, but quite a classic on Risk Management, was the case of the Denver Airport, which opened 15 months later because of a single software program[18].

---

[18] See the case study explained on appendix III. Denver Airport (Case Study)

The worst image a Project Manager would outcast is when happens something like this and he did not anticipate a bit. We see him nervous, improvising, alarming others, pushing the *crisis button*. Effective Project Managers want problems, but they don't want crisis. They want to see problems coming and to have a response already planned. They hate improvising. Any Project Manager should know that he is going to be judged badly if an unpredicted big problem happens. To avoid this awful image, the only thing you can do is to anticipate, to get every risk properly registered before it happens, when it is merely an abstraction. And more important: You have to communicate risks.

The whole group of stakeholders, specially the risk management committee, the steering committee, the PMO, etc., have to be aware of threats, of their importance and the planned response should they happen.

Effective Project Managers don't communicate uncertainty using a tone of complaining or fear. They communicate risks with an approach of maturity and objectivity. Their favorite phrase sounds like this:

"Do we <u>have the right to believe</u> this will go this way? If not, we should anticipate by executing these activities effectively."

This expression "Do we have the right to believe…" for me is the key word to enter on risk management effectively.

We owe Tom DeMarco the relationship between Risk Management and "The Right to Believe". Tom DeMarco defines risk management this way:

> *Risk management is the business of believing only what you have a right to believe*

If the Project Manager get to manage risks this way, there is a win-win result:

- The Project Manager wins because nobody is going to blame him unfairly.
- The project wins because the best actions can be taken when there is time to execute.

4.5 Habit 5. Communicating (Empathic Listening)

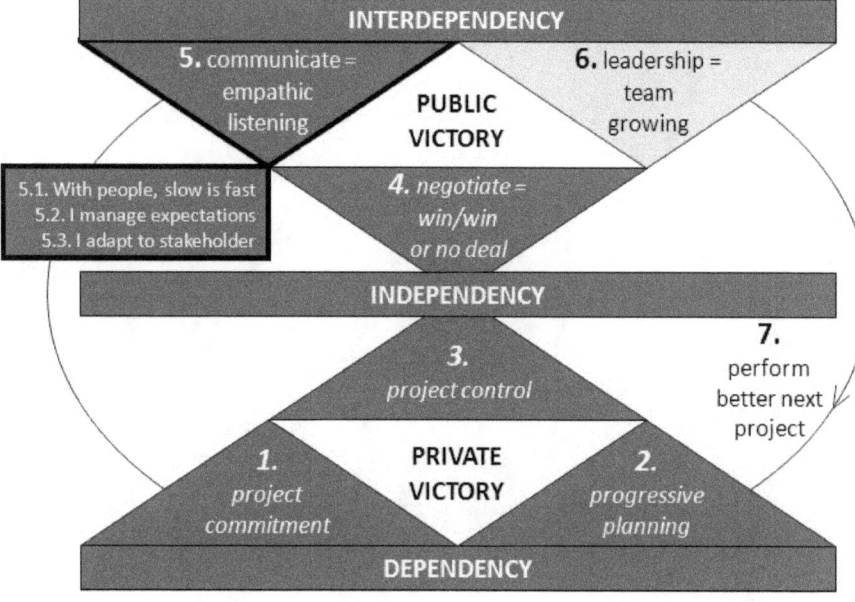

Most conversations are simply monologues delivered in the presence of a witness

MARGARET MILLER

I'm sorry I could not have written a shorter letter, but I didn't have the time

ABRAHAM LINCOLN

4. The Habits of Effective Project Managers

The 5th Habit of Effective People: Seek First to Understand then to be Understood

The fifth habit of highly effective people, according to Covey is "seek first to understand then to be understood". In an effective conversation, *we would use ears twice as much as mouth*, but we generally talk twice as much as we listen. We tend you listen just to prepare our response, not to understand. If somebody tells us a problem, we tend to proscribe the solution that served us, assuming our biography is representative and valid enough for others. *We tell the myopic to put our glasses.*

According to Covey, because we listen autobiographically, we tend to respond in one of four ways. It is important to be aware if we are using one of those four patterns to recognize we are not communicating effectively:

- **Evaluate**: We either agree or disagree.
- **Probe**: We ask questions from our own frame of reference.
- **Advise**: We give counsel based on our own experience.
- **Interpret**: We try to figure people out, to explain their motives, their behavior, based on our own motives and behavior.

> *The four autobiographical responses: evaluate, probe, advise and interpret*

Effective communication occurs when we take our time to really understand the other person, empathetically, being on his/her shoes. We should not give our response if we don't understand well. This has to be done in a true way, without manipulating, investing funds in the *Emotional Bank Account*.

This true communication has more to do with character than with skills. Anyway, there are some skills we could try to get this empathic communication. Covey explained this through a very eloquent example: a conversation between a father and his son. According to Covey, there are four levels of empathic communication, from lower to higher effectiveness:

- **To mimic content**: The son says "Boy, Dad, I've had it! School is for the birds!" and the father responds "You've had it. You think school is for the birds". This is the skill taught in "active" or "reflective" listening. Without the character and relationship base, it is often insulting to people and causes them to close up. It is, however, a first-stage skill because it at least causes you to listen to what's being said. Mimicking content is easy. The father just listens to the words that come out of the son's mouth and he repeats them. He's hardly even using his brain at all. He has essentially repeated back the content of what the son has said. He hasn't evaluated or probed or advised or interpreted. He's at least showed he's paying attention to the son's words.

- **To rephrase the content**: The son says "Boy, Dad, I've had it! School is for the birds!" and the father responds "You don't want to go to school anymore". This time, the father has just put the son's meaning into his own words. He is thinking about what the son said, mostly with the left side, the reasoning, logical side of the brain.

▪ **To reflect feeling**: The son says "Boy, Dad, I've had it! School is for the birds!" and the father responds "You're feeling really frustrated". The father is not paying as much attention to what the son is saying as to the way he feels about what the son is saying.

▪ **To rephrase the content and reflect the feeling**: The son says "Boy, Dad, I've had it! School is for the birds!" and the father responds "You're really frustrated about school". Frustration is the feeling; school is the content. The father is using both sides of his brain to understand son's communication. As the father authentically seeks to understand, as he rephrases content and reflect feeling, he is giving psychological air to his son. He also helps his son work through his own thoughts and feelings: The son is not thinking and feeling one thing and communicating another. He begins to trust his father with his innermost tender feelings and thoughts.

Habit 4 (Win-Win or No Deal) and 5 (Seek First to Understand then to be Understood) are tightly linked. Effective communication is the cornerstone to reach win-win agreements. Those third alternatives are only found when we seek the solution together, when the parties are communicating effectively.

> *Effective communication is the cornerstone to reach*
> *Win-Win agreements*

We cannot control what the other person thinks. We only could to follow this process of five steps to try to get effective agreements based on effective communication:

1. **To show that we are trustworthy**: Opening with phrases as "Can we go for a solution that is better than mine or yours? It's very important that we maintain our good relationship. If we don't get a mutual beneficial agreement, would you mind if we conclude No Deal?"

2. **To seek to understand** (empathic listening, rephrasing content and reflecting feeling): With phrases as "It seems we have different opinions on this. I need to listen to you. Please explain me your point with all details."

3. **To be understood**: With phrases as "Now. Would you be willing to listen to me the way I listened to you?" While we are explaining our point, the other has the right to intervene —we cannot oblige the other to listen empathically.

4. **To probe solutions**: Previous to start probing solutions, it's good to set the rule that we are not allowed to go back to define the problem again. In this phase we have to collaborate as a team, with the problem ahead, actively seeking for alternatives. It's sure there are better solutions than each part could find on their own.

5. **To close on agreements**: Finally, it is important to close agreements and the way to operate for each part. Especially important is to check everybody wins.

The 5th Habit of Effective Project Managers: Communicate = Empathic Listening

Effective Project Managers give great importance to communication. PMI® tells us that it is normal to devote to communicating over 90% of your time. That is, most of the time, you should be writing emails, reports, memos and other documents, reviewing, distributing and storing these documents, etc. Communication is not only written. Most part of the time is consumed in calls, instant messaging, videoconferencing, presenting, meetings with, customer, managers and the rest of stakeholders, individually with team members to provide clarify expectations and provide feedback, not to mention the informal communication that takes place in the hallways, in the dining room, in front of the coffee machine, etc.

An Effective Project Manager should master many techniques related to communication. He would seem ineffective if he is not proficient on form (i.e. he saturates audience with rambling texts, or his texts lack structure, synthesis or grammatical correctness). He also would seem ineffective because of the process (i.e. he arranges a project meeting without a clear agenda, closes the meeting without agreeing on next steps, his minutes don't reflect what was said properly). Techniques have to be mastered: they necessary but not sufficient for effective communication.

To me, effective communication *is more an art than a science*. Effective communication is more complex in Project Management than in Operations Management. There are many courses, books and other educational material to learn how to communicate, but nothing is as instructive and eloquent as the living example some people provide in their daily work. I've learned a lot from these Project Managers *true artists of effective communication*. When I say this I always think of my appreciated colleague Joan.

We can consider that Joan and I work in a virtual project team (much phone, much email). We live in distant cities hundreds of kilometers apart. This project lasts over a year. He is the Project Manager. I'm one of the main stakeholders —in a power-interest grid, I would have much power, much interest.

I have to admit that I often cause much saturation in the tam when I ask for new requirements. I have no patience with the response times and I get despair at poor testing. Despite all these obsessions of mine, I've never had to complain to his boss. When there has been an issue that I could have managed on my own without informing him, I've preferred to ask him, even if it took me longer. And what is perhaps most striking: I don't remember a discussion with Joan. How does he do it?

I know Joan has received much training on social skills. However, in my opinion, its effectiveness is not explained by their mastery of the theory and communication techniques. Joan is a great communicator for other reasons:

- He maintains a positive attitude. He is honesty and respectful to everyone.
- He is not afraid to deliver bad news.
- He always prefers talking to other communication channels. He's a great conversationalist. He's always looking for occasions to get in touch.
- When talking with you, he gives you priority on others. You get his all attention, no time limit. His calls take more than 30 minutes.
- He seeks to understand rephrasing with his own words. You feel he is trying to get on your shoes. He truly tries to understand before to be understood. He will later convince you of his solution, which surely he has thought at the beginning. But if your solution is better for the project, he will accept without hesitation.

Many people would think that Joan spends too much time talking, but for those who know him well, Joan is an Effective Project Manager: He consistently delivers on time, on cost, on scope, with good quality. That 90% of the time we spend communicating, if we use it well, is the major cause of success in projects. To be like Joan you have to master the habit of empathetic listening. The fifth habit of highly effective people "seek first to understand then to be understood" could be translated this way to the field of Project Management:

- **5.1) With people, Slow is Fast**: When talking with you, Joan is never in a hurry. As Covey said: *With people, slow is fast, and fast is slow*. If you want people do what you say just by ordering, using them as interchangeable things of a machine, with the industrial era mindset, then you should not manage projects. Joan makes frequent deposits in the Emotional Bank Account, not only as 30 minutes calls, also by email, instant messaging, etc. This way he gets trustworthy. When someone want to argue with him, he easily confront the problem taking distance from the problem, not from the person, being objective, giving more importance to project goals, convincing, not imposing. Before an important meeting, he has had that meeting with each stakeholder separately.

- **5.2) I Manage Expectations**: If a project is poorly sold, it hardly will be a success. When Joan manages one of these projects, he try to manage stakeholder's expectations to provide not what they ask but what they need. In order to infer real requisites, he uses effective communication.

- **5.3) I adapt my Communication to Stakeholders**: With each stakeholder, Joan uses a proper language: technical language with technical people, business language with managers, etc..

5.1) With People, Slow is Fast

Effective communication is based on effective listening, that is, the ability to empathize, to stand in the other's shoes. Empathize does not mean to agree: we just want to see reality from his point of view to understand him better.

Effective Project Managers try to guess what's behind the apparent communication, what's hidden, what's the basis for the other's message. Two PMBOK® processes are related to this: *10.1 Identify Stakeholders* and *10.4 Manage Stakeholders Expectations*. If we just focus on the standard, it would seem sufficient to have a determined strategy to manage each person. This sounds a bit manipulative —and ineffective for the project in the long run. In practice, I think that my responsibility as a Project Manager is to get to know well each stakeholder, putting myself on his or her place regarding the project. This attitude demands frequent deposits on Emotional Bank Accounts: I have to go slowly with everyone. I should know about their interests, who I need to make more happy and how. There are no recipes again to do this: just the habit of empathic communication.

Regarding stakeholder communication management, there is a field where we need to go slower: when we have conflicts and arguments.

Effective Project Managers are not afraid of conflicts among team members, among stakeholders, or when they directly confront us. They see these as *golden* opportunities to public victories for the project sake. Solved project conflicts are good for Project Managers (they look effective) but also good for the project since stakeholder community is aware of a qualitative improvement when the solution satisfies the parties involved.

Should we Project Managers learn some Psychology? That wouldn't do any harm. Following I will try to describe a psychological theory I have put into practice with good results. It allows me to explain "why people argue".

Even better, when it's me the one involved in the argument, it allows me to take distance from emotion: I think there are situational patterns and common solutions. What happen to me has happened to much more people before. According Canadian psychiatrist Eric Berne, who developed the theory known as **Transactional Analysis**, published in 1964 within his famous book *Games People Play: The Psychology of Human Relationships*, when people communicate, they basically interact from three ego-states: the parent "me", the adult "me", and the child "me".

When I draw these three ego-states with circles one above the other, the figure reminds me of a snowman:

Transactional Analysis Theory, Eric Berne (1910-1970)

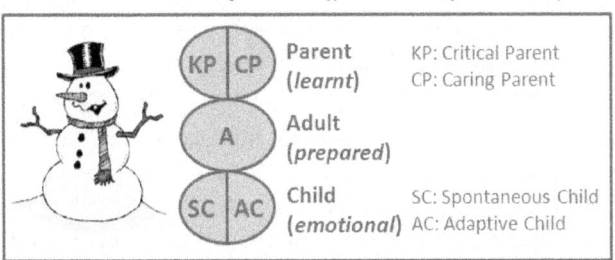

Parent (*learnt*)	KP: Critical Parent
	CP: Caring Parent
Adult (*prepared*)	
Child (*emotional*)	SC: Spontaneous Child
	AC: Adaptive Child

Parallel transaction → Dialogue   Crossed transaction → Argument
Confronting conflicts → A-A

- The **parent "me"** represents norms rules and attitudes. All the opinions about right and wrong, how we should behave and how we should act are represented here, along with all the "musts" and "nos", praise and encouragement. We take our parental self from our childhood so it is linked strongly to the environment we grew up in. The parental "me" can be divided into two parts. There is a critical, authoritarian side which sets limits and gives warnings (critical parent –KP-). The other part is the caring side which encourages and helps (caring parent –CP-).

- The **adult "me"** contains our ability to think independently, without being affected by our adult or child selves other tan to receive information from them. The adult self makes rational decisions, collects information, analyses, refines and assesses probability. This self is logical, objective and free of prejudice. Another way of describing this "me" is to call it your computer.

- The **child "me"** contains our feelings and needs. When we are little we act spontaneously (spontaneous child –SC-) and emotionally (adaptive child –AC-) to get what we want and need. Our creativity resides in the child self, along with our ability to laugh, cry, love and hate. If we are unhappy the cause can usually be found in the child "me" in the form of repressed or unsatisfied needs and emotions.

According to **Transactional Analysis**, when people communicate, the message sender uses one of his "me" to head the receiver "me": that is a transaction. When receiver responds, that is another transaction:

- True communication occurs when transactions are parallel. Parallel transaction builds agreement. It can continue, in principle, indefinitely. Example: One person criticizes other (KP→AC) and the other responds admitting the critic and apologizing (AC→KP).

- There is an argument when transactions are crossed. A crossed transaction is based on the fact that you are in different "me" states and communication is broken. Example: One person criticizes other (KP→AC) and the other responds backfiring (KP→AC).

- It will be difficult to resolve a crossed transaction constructively unless one of the parties changes its communication mode. Usually, the one who wins the transactional game is the one who gets into his adult "me" to head the adult "me" of the other (A→A).

> *Confront conflicts using your adult "me"*

Let's illustrate the theory by setting some examples. Let's imagine two people waiting in the cinema line:

- *This is typical! Long queues and no service. No-one cares about the customer anymore!*

- *You are absolutely right! And that's not all...*

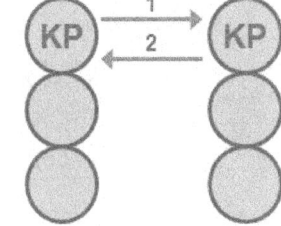

There is no argument in this case. Instead, they will probably continue talking animatedly until the movie starts.

Now imagine an employee asking for advice to her boss:

- *Do you have any comments or opinions about my work?*

- *I think there are quite a few things that could improve. What about...*

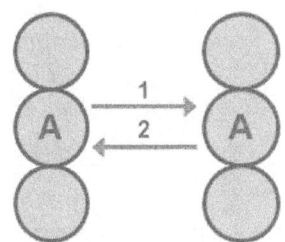

Here we are two people talking respectfully in a professional way. They are not likely to have an argument.

Boss and employee don't have an argument neither in this sequence:

- *Help! I cannot manage. I feel useless.*

- *Here, let me do it for you. You need rest.*

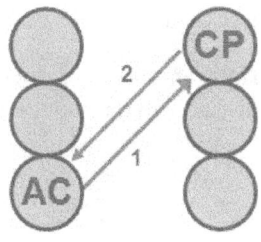

Now the opposite example in which there is an argument. It's me coming home asking something to my wife:

- *What's for dinner?*

- *So typical of you getting home late and making me hurry! Do you want me to start preparing dinner right now? I was about to take a break from kids...*

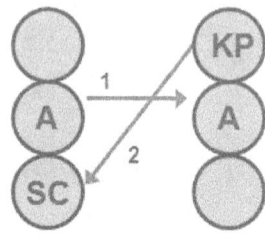

Oops! Now I better resolve the transaction constructively to *win the transactional game* (I recalled A→A):

- *I'm sorry, darling. I just asked to give a hand. I didn't know you were taking a break. Did you have a hard day with the children? Did they misbehave?*

- *Yes, they have. It's been a long day. Let me take a break, please. Meanwhile, you could prepare the salad...*

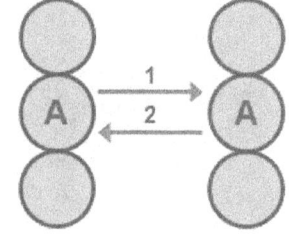

Do you see how the theory works? It's not about *manipulating people*. It's just about to know how to communicate effectively.

Knowing there are theories explaining what happen to us is useful to take distance from emotions, which is really necessary sometimes...

I remember once when I opened my email inbox to find an email from my boss like this:

> "Jose, how do you happen to postpone the meeting with this client we are chasing for so long? Didn't it worth making an effort?"

You could not imagine how offended I felt by that short line "how do you happen to..." I hardly could keep on reading. I took this as a formidable lack of respect. He did not even say good morning! It's really incredible how offensive certain phrases can be.

If I let go myself on that very minute, I would have responded by email, with very bad manners. But then I recalled the advice I got at a recent course on human skills. I remembered there were communication patterns: *You should not respond by email when you are upset*. It also made me took "psychological air" to be aware that my boss was using a transaction of the kind KP→SC. So I thought:

> My boss is using his "critical parent" to head my "spontaneous child."

I was aware of the communication pattern I was in. I took distance and calm myself down almost immediately. Then I decided to *respond*, better than *react*. I recalled that the most effective response was to use transactional pattern A→A (i.e. adult to adult).

I quickly elaborated a kind response, in an objective factual tone, explaining the situation and the logic behind, without criticizing anybody. I hit the "send" button, ditched the issue on my side at once, and I focused on the work ahead and other more important things.

Since I experienced that, I give importance to communication patterns. They serve us to understand better people and ourselves. If we use them well, they give us effectiveness in our projects.

Another communication pattern I find extraordinary useful is this feedback rule number 1: Don't say "you", say "I".

> *The feedback rule #1:*
> *Don't say "you", say "I"*

As Project Managers, we often have the responsibility of telling some team member, colleague, seller, etc. that he is not doing well a thing.

On these occasions, we should overcome many cultural and educational stereotypes. When we think about someone, we tend to label him with adjectives. We are not use to thinking "Jose is being delayed 15 minutes" instead we think "Jose is always late". If we want Jose improve punctuality and we tell him that he is an unpunctual person, we will feel offended, become defensive, and we'll have an argument. Jose could backfire on his side with phrases like:

- *You don't know what happened. Why do you criticize me?*
- *You have never been late?*
- *I'm just 10 minutes late. What's your idea of being unpunctual?*
- *I beg your pardon? What did you call me? Are you insulting me?*
- *Don't you shout me!*

Most likely, we finish by discussing issues of form rather than substance. There will be no effective communication for sure. Conversely, if we speak in the first person, saying what we feel and believe by ourselves, then what we say is less arguable and there will be more opportunities for effective communication. See how communication changes if instead of labeling Jose as unpunctual, we say something like this:

- *On this morning meeting with the customer I got so nervous and irritated when you don't turned up on time. I think it took 15 minutes without any signal from you. I think we have given a bad image. In future I want you to warn me when you think you are coming late, please.*

Jose may agree or disagree, but he is not going to discuss if this is true or false. This is what you think, and it is out of question.

In my courses, I ask students to do the following exercise: Reformulate these phrases so that they start not by "you" but "I"

1. *You're lying.*
2. *You're forgetting something.*
3. *You're wrong.*
4. *You're being illogical.*
5. *You're wandering from the point.*
6. *You're not explaining properly*
7. *You've got to learn to be punctual.*
8. *You must inform people better.*

After a short time, they usually produce phrases like these:

1. *I don't believe that piece of information can be correct.*
2. *I'd like to add something.*
3. *I don't see things in the same light as you.*
4. *I find it difficult to follow your reasoning.*
5. *I don't see what that's got to do with the problem we're trying to solve.*
6. *I don't understand what you mean.*
7. *I get so (irritated, infuriated, angry) when you don't turn up on time.*
8. *In future I want you to tell people about the following points...*

5.2) I Manage Expectations

Effective Project Managers know very well that stakeholders' management is the most important project knowledge area. *A project only finishes when stakeholders have met or exceeded their expectations.* That is: when they are *happy with the project result.*

Each project has many stakeholders, but one of them especially important to manage: the **client**[19], the one who pays for it —we should extend this group of special interest with **final user**s, the ones who are to use the product, service or result. If we don't get client actively interested in our project during execution, or gets surprised or upset with the final result, then our project will be a great failure.

One boss of mine used to say: "In projects, client has to be happy with everything but the price."

---

[19] In many service oriented companies is usual that the person who sold the project tries to centralize communication with the client. Effective Project Managers do their best to manage client expectations by themselves with the least intermediation.

"Getting client happy with everything" is easier said than done. What techniques do we need? The top of the iceberg is effective communication, but on the base we have all the project knowledge, standards like PMBOK®, all the experience and lessons learned. This is a list of some expectations clients usually have on each project knowledge area:

- **Integration Management** is important for them: Clients and users see the Project Manager as the single point of contact and the main source of information. Project Managers centralize issue and change management, the process, the results and project management overall.

- **Scope Management**: They expect us to manage requirements, being able to distinguish what they ask from what they really need, reconciling real needs with project objectives.

- **Schedule and Cost Management**: Clients need project results quickly and cheap.

- **Quality Management**: We will fail if we deliver a product that clients and users perceive as "poor quality".

- **Resources Management**: They know that results are better with good professionals working right.

- **Communication Management**: Communication is the way we relate each other. Until you deliver the product, or a part of it, the only thing stakeholders can see is communication.

- **Risk Management**: Clients don't like crisis.

- **Procurement Management**: We may subcontract other parties, but in face of the client we are prime responsible.

In conclusion, "getting the client happy with everything" has very much to do with everything related to Project Management. Where do we need to focus communication, then?

To the best of my knowledge, the habit of managing expectations has to be especially trained in two fronts: **1) Change Management** (don't confuse with issue management) and **2) Quality Management**.

Managing Change Expectations

Quite often, projects are performed to set up change in organizations. When implementing a product, service or any other final result into the performing organization, chances are we are introducing big changes in the daily work of much people, whose natural fear to change can be a serious threat to project goals.

Effective Project Managers should foresee how the transformation components of a project will affect these people —and also the subsequent changes in operation phases after the project. Changes should not be "sold" to people who are going to change on the merits of the *new status quo*. People don't leave easily their comfort zone. They act more emotional than rational.

People Hate Change

Better than praising the advantages in the new future scenario after the project, it is much more effective if you focus on how bad is the situation now, to get people aware of the inconveniences of keeping the same. Can we afford not doing the project? This rationale serves to get the project buy in, and anyone involved have to be aware of it. Then you have to sell not the long term advantages of the new scenario, but the short term convenience of the project you are executing right now. In this stage, it is not important for them to visualize that long term future (although it is useful for you).

When starting changes during the project, you have to expect people to be uneasy with this phase of "chaos" —they feel insecure because you are forcing them back to the uncomfortable position of novice in some part of their work.

If then you explain and try to sell the merits of the new scenario, they simply won't listen. You should offer them something they understand as a quick remedy to the chaotic situation. Your project scope should include some element to provide some order (transforming idea). In your plan this could be just the first step of a series. You don't need to communicate everything. Just stuck to what they need to know now.

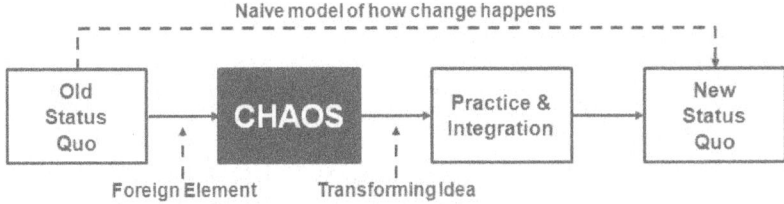

To give an example, think of the physicians' opposition that could threat a project named "Paperless Hospital". Imagine they are already in "chaos mode" because they know that at the end of the project they will not be allowed to keep the paper medical files. Could it be effective to anticipate the system functionality making them start prescribing by computer? Incidentally, they will start watching screens and menu options, entering data for prescriptions... In short, they get familiar with the new system. This could be much more effective than convincing them on the great advancements of electronic medical records, backup systems, enterprise master patient indexes, HL7 protocol for information change system to system, etc. To all of these they will simply not listen.

Managing Quality Expectations

Final customer satisfaction cannot be quick fixed or improvised. It has to be worked on continuously. We say quality is planned, designed, and built in —not inspected in. We need to anticipate acceptance criteria, to set quality assurance and quality control processes that make more probable those acceptance criteria are met. However, we get frustrated when clients don't close requirements. What should we do then to manage quality expectations?

Imagine you lead a software development project. You gather requirements first moth. Your team work at your venues for six months, then final release is delivered. You have been very efficient but, have you been effective?

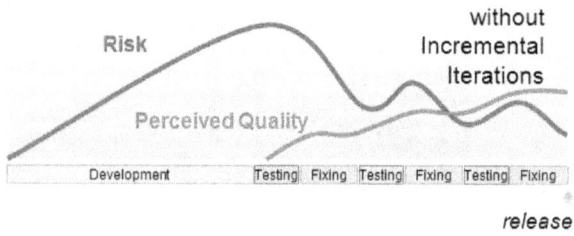

The client will see the product first time on month seven. Chances are it doesn't match precisely with his idea. He submits a non-acceptance report for 80% of features. Next iterations of software testing and fixing don't raise the product up to acceptable levels of perceived quality. The day of go-live comes but it's impossible to reduce the defect rate to get client acceptance.

If we could measure project risk, we'll see much cumulated risk exposure until release date. Through the testing phase it is not possible to reduce effectively the risk level. On the other hand, until release date quality perceived is zero. When product is first time received quality perceived goes up but don't reach the level to pass acceptance criteria.

Now imagine you practice an incremental iterative lifecycle approach. Let's see how you can improve your client quality expectations management.

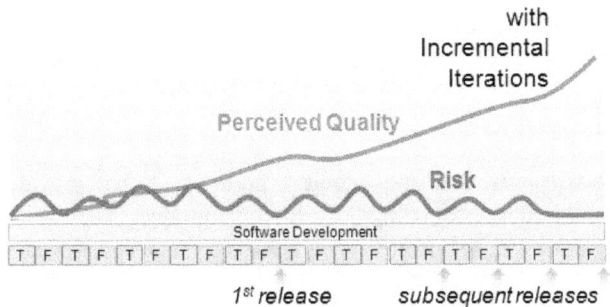

After each iteration (or sprint) you build something that can be tested, fixed and demonstrated to the client. Perceived quality is increasing since the beginning, and risk exposure levels keep always under control. After some iterations you deliver a first release of a part of the system they could use. The figure shows three subsequent releases. The last fifth will serve to formal closure of the project.

Each time you deliver, the client reformulates his own idea of the product. He is likely to change some requirements. He says: "This is good, but..." and then he enumerates a series of items to be changed. Next release you deliver what he has asked for, and he surely is not discussing that again. He will discuss other things, fewer each time. In Projects with high level of risks, it's very effective to manage quality by means of incremental iterations. This is just common sense risk management.

Common Sense Risk Management: If we get the client to say 20 times "Yes, but..." then last time is not going to say "No"

---

4. The Habits of Effective Project Managers

Iterative incremental project management approach requires a very careful plan, developed well in advance, for what will be in each and every increment. Functional items are ordered according the value delivered to the stakeholders, the need to confirm risk assumptions, etc. Least important items are scheduled for last releases. This way, if the project is early canceled, or deadline is moved before expected, you could close on valuable delivered releases.

Since first deliveries (final subsystems or prototypes) users provide positive and negative feedback. Little by little, the final product is approaching what they really need. Project effort value is constantly well appreciated.

5.3) I adapt my Communication to Stakeholders

We human beings are different from animals in many aspects, of course. Maybe one of the most differential is our need to communicate, especially when something concerns us deeply and we see it as a threat, or a substantial change. We are information consumers. We eat information. As a species, we could be called *informivore*.

When we are hungry of information, we expect the worst, especially in projects. We think something is going wrong. Apart from gossips and misunderstandings, we have plenty of own past experiences to feed our worst fears and negative expectations.

Information is power, but is not ethical (nor effective) to hide information to avoid problems. We should not be afraid to deliver bad news. We will be judged as ineffective if our communication is not clear, concise, complete, timely, relevant, compelling, predictable, reliable, confidential, etc.

Especially, we will be heavily criticized if our communication is not clear and concise:

- If information is concise but confusing (like some emails of two lapidary phrases) then stakeholders will panic. They will distrust us, asking directly to our bosses.
- If information is clear but cumbersome, then stakeholders won't read. They will respond endless emails asking what they need to know again and again. When they get the information through other channels, they will see us as replaceable.
- If cumbersome and confusing, then we look inept and will cause much frustration among stakeholders.

Therefore, effective communication should be clear and concise. It's worth more time writing so that stakeholders spend less time reading. Nevertheless, we can communicate that way and not being effective yet. Effective Project Managers have the habit of adapting their communication to stakeholders.

In my projects, I'm used to seeing stakeholders as "mouths to be fed". Until the team delivers some product, the only thing stakeholders I have to serve them is communication.

> *Until you deliver the product, or a part of it, the only*
> *thing stakeholders can see is communication*

If we applied methods from the industrial age to manage projects, then communication would be another area to optimize. In culinary terms: "We would serve the same cheeseburger for everyone".

Regarding projects, I like to think that all stakeholders need "to eat information" but their diets vary: PMOs eat weekly complete status reports; steering committee eats biweekly risk reports, CFO eats actual costs, variances and forecasting reports, etc.

When we have "*informivores*" (a.k.a. stakeholders) sitting at our restaurant (a.k.a. project) we have to get them satisfied:

- You have to ask them what shall they have to dinner —they may order a *cheeseburger*, but you don't decide this. In regard to projects, this means agreeing on their communication requirements, what they need to be informed on what format, etc.

- You have to tell them how long it will take to get served, and take this as a promise to keep. In projects, this is a communication plan indicating for instance that there will be a weekly status report by email. There is nothing more frustrating for stakeholders than sporadic unpredictable communication. Sticking to the plan is effective: You spare a lot of questions from stakeholders —they know that answers are coming when promised.

- You want them to become regular customers. You have to ask them if everything was to their liking. That is asking for stakeholder feedback on our communication management process.

4.6 Habit 6. Leadership (Team Growing)

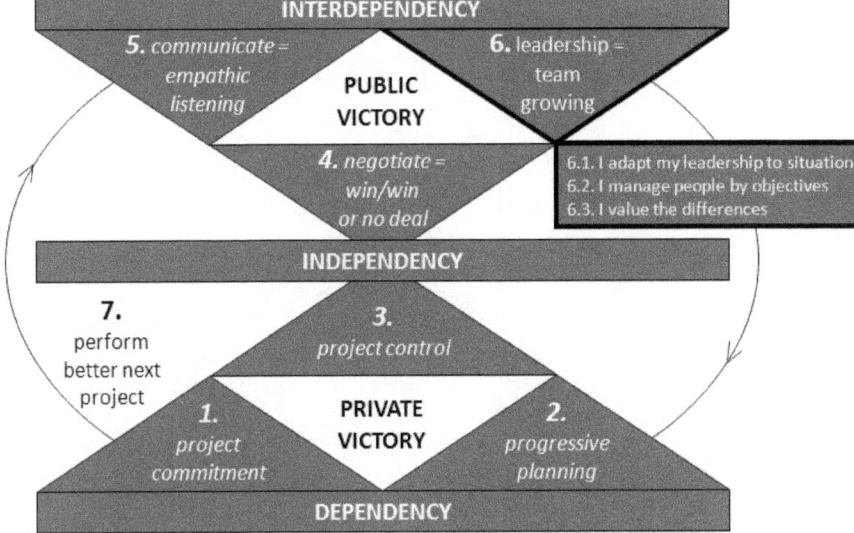

Bad leaders are hated. Mediocre ones are obeyed.
A leader is best when people barely know he exists
When his work is done, his aim fulfilled,
they will say: we did it ourselves

LAO-TZU

4. The Habits of Effective Project Managers

The 6th Habit of Effective People: Synergize

The sixth habit of highly effective people, according to Covey is "synergize". Synergy is a principle[20]. Simply defined, it means that the whole is greater than the sum of its parts. Two pieces of wood will hold much more than the double of the weight. If you plant two plants close together, the roots commingle and improve the quality of the soil so that both plants will grow better. Synergy is the habit of most hierarchy. It is the key to public victories.

We need a lot of self-esteem to get aware that in this interdependent world we won't get away by ourselves. *No one can whistle a symphony. It takes an orchestra to play it.* Worthy challenges are achieved only by working together.

Working as a team, the weaknesses of one are compensated by the strength of the others, but the result is greater than the sum of the parts. Every problem has a solution, but not just one or two, but many. *We see the world not as it is, but as we are.* When we work together, with the problem ahead, we discover third alternatives unreachable separately.

Significant creativity would not happen if we all thought alike. It is necessary (and great!) that people are different. The possibilities of human intelligence multiply in creative cooperation.

After a synergic experience, one is not the same anymore. There is a before and an after.

---

[20] Other principles are, to name a few: responsibility, respect, fairness, honesty, integrity, dignity, humbleness, loyalty, temperance, encouragement, excellence, contribution, patience, potential, growth, compassion, etc.

The 6th Habit of Effective Project Managers: Leadership = Team Growing (The Law of the Harvest)

Effectiveness in projects is a collective result. Synergy in projects has much to do with "team leadership". A Project Manager wants his team do voluntarily what he wants: that is, to achieve the project goals. Just being appointed as Project Manager is not enough to get this.

You may say you are leading, but if team members don't follow you, if they don't do willingly what you ask, then you are not a leader for them. Why would people follow? They don't follow you because you're clever or because you're always right. Keep this in mind: They follow you *because they love you.*

As a Project Manager, you don't build a team like building a wall using bricks, just by following a certain process. You can't make teams built, you can hope they will become a synergic team; you can act to improve the odds of team building; but you can't make it happen at all. The process is much too fragile to be controlled.

Think of agriculture. This is a fair model closer enough to how team formation works. Agriculture isn't entirely controllable. Instead of saying "team building" we should say "team growing". This expression reminds the law of the harvest.

> *There is no "team building", there is only "team growing"*

The farmer enriches the soil, plants the seeds, waters according to the latest theory, and then he holds his breath. He just might get a crop; he might not. If the last minute he has a hailstorm, he will lose his work. If it all comes up roses, he'll feel fine, but next year he will cross fingers again.

What a Project Manager can do for *team growing*, apart from crossing fingers? He can apply a principle centered leadership. The complete person paradigm can be applied to the individual (grow the body, the mind, the heart and the spirit) but we can also apply this paradigm to leading teams. An effective leader should play **the four roles of principle centered leadership**:

- **Modeling** (related with the spirit, or corporative conscience): To be a model of integrity and a reference to others. To inspire trust.

- **Pathfinding** (related with the mind, or strategic vision): Not to impose a way of doing things, but to consider advice and recommendations from others. To find third ways with them to get involved emotionally.

- **Aligning** (related with the body, or discipline): Institutionalize processes, structure and systems, in order to homogenize work at the corporate level.

- **Empowering** (related with the heart, or passion): By focusing on the result, delegate work to people, according to their skills, to get them grow professionally and help them find *their own voice*.

The above applies to leadership in a broad sense. These four roles of leadership can be applied to Project Management too, but they don't guarantee success: Project success highly depends on the project team.

If team members are not skilled, or they are not goal oriented, or simply they don't get along, then we can be certain that project goals are not going to be achieved, no matter what the Project Manager does. The Project Manager is nothing without a team. The "complete person" paradigm is not enough here. We another paradigm: the "complete team" paradigm.

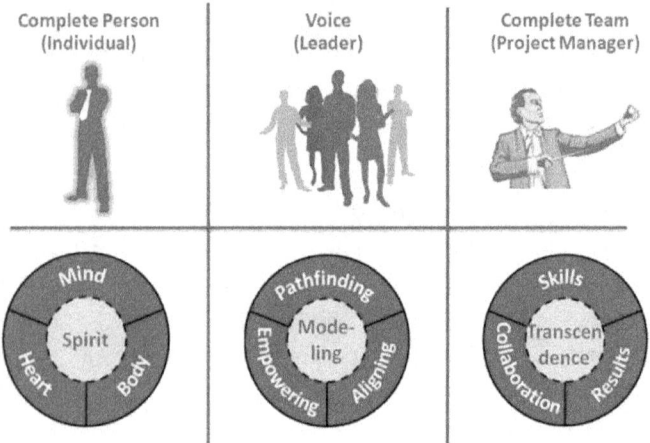

The sixth habit of highly effective people "synergize" could be translated this way to the field of Project Management:

- **6.1) I Adapt My Leadership to Situation**: Since the beginning of the project, I have delegation in mind.
- **6.2) I Manage People by Objectives**: I control people not by the working hours they put, but the results they achieve.
- **6.3) I Value the Differences**: I need a complete team balancing collaboration, skills and orientation to results. I have two project results in mind: the product and the team.

6.1) I Adapt my Leadership Style to Situation

Traditionally there have always been two styles of leadership: The democratic leader (people oriented) and the authoritarian leader (result oriented). In 1972, authors Paul Hersey and Kenneth Blanchard published their book "Management of organizational behavior: utilizing human resources" (now on its 10th edition) on the interesting idea that leadership is effective only when adapted to team maturity.

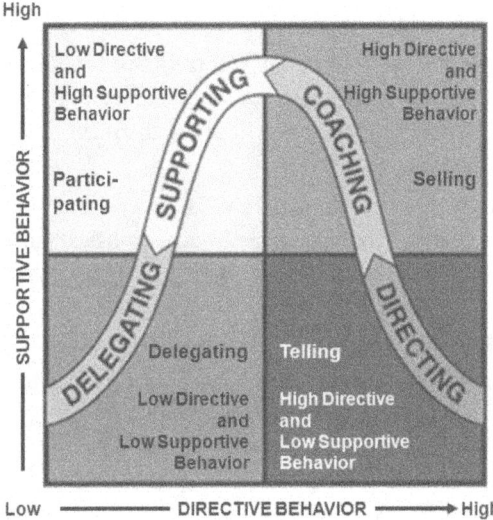

According to this theory, there is no better style of leadership. In order to be effective as a leader, you have to adapt your leadership style to the capability of the team on getting results and taking work ownership.

If we could measure how much is the leader involved on tasks (horizontal axis "*directive behavior*": providing directions on how each task has to be done to get results) and we also could measure how much is the leader concerned about people (vertical axis "*supportive behavior*": helping people to develop), this theory tell us there is a sequential path (if maturity goes backward then we have to repeat the phases again). Since the teamwork begins until they are self-sufficient, the leader may use these four styles:

- **Directing** (Telling): The leader defines the roles of the team and provides the what, how, why, when and where to do the task.

- **Coaching** (Selling): While the leader is still providing the direction, he or she is now using two-way communication and providing the socio-emotional support that will allow the team being influenced to buy into the process.

- **Supporting** (Participating): This is how shared decision-making about aspects of how the task is accomplished and the leader is providing less task behaviors while maintaining high relationship behavior.

- **Delegating**: The leader is still involved in decisions; however, the process and responsibility has been passed to the team. The leader stays involved to monitor progress.

Effective Project Managers should have the habit of delegating. They need self-sufficient teams to focus on management. Team members are not autonomous at the beginning (they depend very much on Project Manager), but with the time they have to be autonomous. The Project Manager will be able to delegate almost completely, and this is good for the project goals.

I learnt this from a team that became self-sufficient not because of me, *but in spite of me.*

In the year 2000, a company in the industry of pay per view TV services contracted us a project. The main objective was that customers may reload their electronic wallet cards by means of TV appliances. We had to develop the central part of the system: a message broker server centralizing communications with finance entities. This project was named "Electronic Wallet Reloading Server (**EWRS**)".

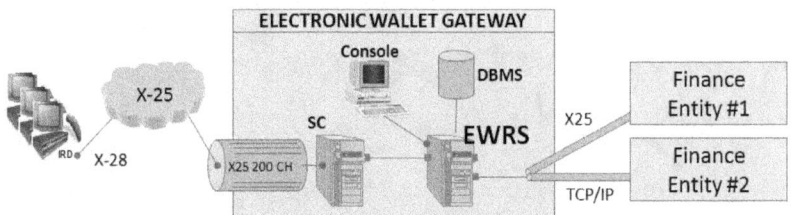

That was a mission critical system (many users, many economic transactions, high cost if the system was not available). Service level required was above 400 concurrent users and above 30 reloads per second. This was a high risk project: The risk register had a lot o risks for technological innovation, technological complexity, third parties' dependence, change management, etc. I strove to manage these risks, but I didn't see the bigger one. In the words of Tom DeMarco: "I took elaborate care not to trip over the railroad ties, but I did not see the oncoming train". In my case, that oncoming train was resource turnover.

My great asset for this project was Fernando, an excellent analyst with I had the pleaser to work in past projects. I didn't know **Eva**, but she came with good references as programmer. **Paloma** would join after vacation (she has no experience on C++ programming, she would learn on the job). Later on, we would recruit another two programmers. We started Fernando, Eva and I with requirement management. When Paloma arrived, she devoted to C++ training. Fernando and I took turns for vacations. When he was back, Fernando told me he quit. When Eva was back from vacation, she told me the same. This was very bad!

Fernando left the company on August. Until October I could not replace him with **Israel** (another excellent analyst). Since I was not bad at C++, I decided getting into it. On the presence of my bosses, I complained a lot, of course, but to be honest, I liked it. Paloma followed strictly my directions and later did the same **Pedro** and **Antonio** (newly hired). The figure below shows the evolution of the organization chart during the six months of the project[21].

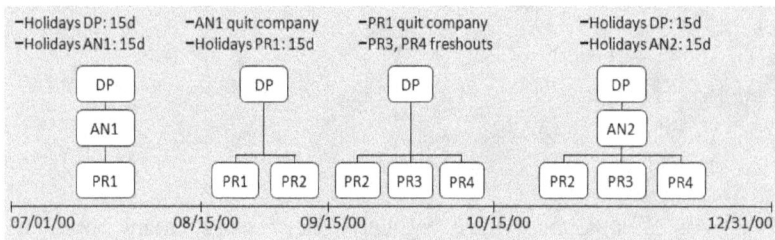

The technical complexity was very high (very stimulating, as well):

- Each transaction (the requirement said 30 per second) implied and average of 20 messages from and to several systems. These messages were not intelligible (they were encoded).

- This was a true real time system. Some logic was dependant of the time (on timeouts exceeded, messages were routed differently). Many times our prototypes failed only after running for several hours at night, when operating system collapsed.

- The external systems to which messages should be sent and received were not ready at the time (in fact, those projects had not even started). So we developed simulators.

---

[21] AN1=Fernando, AN2=Israel, PR1=Eva, PR2=Paloma, PR3=Pedro, PR4=Antonio.

By the time Israel joined, I thought we had completed the first development iteration (focused on system architecture). The main system modules were up and running and programmers (on their own initiative) started to get specialized: Paloma specialized on messages; Pedro on communications and Antonio on the kernel. However, Israel made me see that EWRS was not going to pass requirements as it was: He performed stress testing and checked it was impossible to reach 200 concurrent users and 10 transactions per second. The kernel should be redesigned inside out.

Coaching (*selling*)

I was so much identified with the work we've done (I felt as *the father of the child*) but Israel was technically quite ahead of me. When we discussed on the technical field he always won. To move on, I decided not to discuss on the "how" but on the "why" and "what for", this way we could understand better each other.

With regards to Paloma, she was not advancing at good pace because, as she said "she didn't get used to programming on bytes". It was certainly difficult to program messages on the byte level on a language you are not proficient. Every time she got an hexadecimal character when it was supposed to be other, that got on her nerves because it took too long to fix.

Then, one day we were discussing how to speed up the testing process, she had an idea. She decided to build a program for visual testing. Paloma was very good in visual programming. She asked me one week to adapt some previous work from another project. After that week, on which she was not disturbed, we started to see a change on her attitude: She was not that shy girl fearful to ask questions anymore. She transformed into a fulfilled collaborative professional who enjoyed with her work.

She even got angry when decided something on messages without her approval, or when we did not used her tools to perform message testing. She gained the others' respect. The figure below shows some screens of the program by Paloma to automate message testing. This tool multiplied team productivity, so as quality of deliverables:

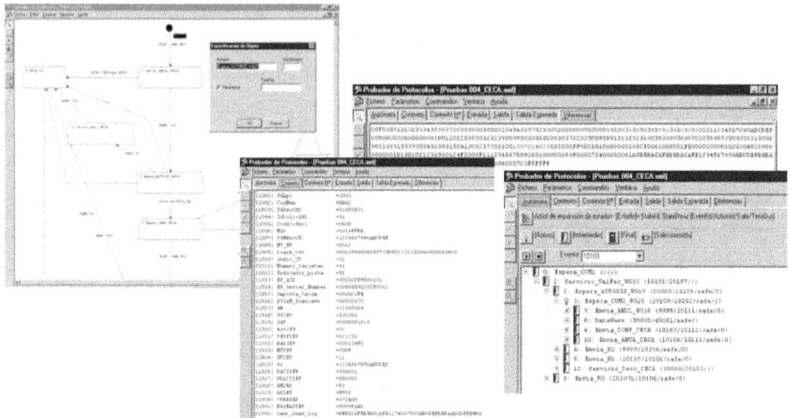

Meanwhile, Pedro and Antonio become effective on their own area of work. When they doubted something, they asked Israel or me. Well, I have to say that *they rather asked Israel.*

I was not aware of that, but the team was going through the phase of "coaching", not because I proactively was adopting the leadership style, but because I had no other choice. Back then I didn't have much experience in project management. My favorite way of managing programmers was to get into their software code. Israel's arrival forced me to change style. I felt very bad about losing control.

Supporting (*participating*)

When Israel was a month into the project, my company assigned me to lead another. It was not a problem for the project because Israel was taking very good, as always. At one point he was alone at follow up meetings. Anyway, if Israel called me, I gave him priority. I was always available when they needed.

I was not aware, but my leadership style had changed to "supporting". When I went to team meetings I felt badly when they used a jargon I didn't follow. I negligently asked them to use a more understandable language, *just in case the client asks me about that*, even though this technical explanation was of no interest to the client.

Delegating

One morning Israel calls me, not to make me go, but to give me the good news: they are finishing on due date. I ask client a meeting to proceed with formal closure. Client tells me that's not possible because the other parties are not even started their projects and he is afraid EWRS will fail when used by them. We agreed a win-win decision: *Client provides an acceptance test inventory. If we pass the tests, then we can close.*

Next morning Israel calls me again: Test inventory proposed by client consists of nearly 200 blocking test cases —if we fail at test case number 50 then we have to start number 1 after fixing. I think they cannot make it. I cancel my compromises and go help.

That afternoon I come to join the team. I keep watching them for a while without being seen: They all were working so focused, in flux state, at full capacity.

There is a board in a corner, in view of all, distinguishing urgent (red), necessary (blue) and convenient tasks (black). Other section entitled "backlog" enumerates pending changes for next release. A big number in a corner says 45 —I guess that's the number of test cases passed. Pedro and Antonio seem to have been in the company for several years. They have really improved in last two months!

This is Israel and I talking at the coffee machine:

—Israel: We were not expecting you here. Something worries you?

—Jose: Client is not leaving us go so easily. That's the reason he push a test phase so hard. If we don't deliver EWRS tomorrow morning, then he will suspect the system is not as ready as I assured, and he will give us another long test inventory to pass, you will see. By the way, how is the testing going?

—Israel: Most of the cases are not new for us. Paloma has prepared a "launcher" to initialize the messages automatically. Pedro and Antonio have adapted the simulators. It didn't take too long to find out 5 cases which failed, some of them impacting kernel classes. When you have arrived we were debugging.

—Jose: If we touch the kernel we need to repeat stress testing, right?

—Israel: Sure.

—Jose: Shall I take it?

—Israel: Ha, ha, ha! That's a good one, Jose!

4. The Habits of Effective Project Managers

When Israel saw I was not kidding, he told me that Antonio was in charge of non functional testing. When he guessed the next thing I'd do was to offer myself to Antonio, he demonstrated me I was technically incapable to perform those tests.

I knew they were going to be working all night. If I couldn't help them with technical tasks, at least I could stay with them giving moral support, buying some pizzas, etc. He didn't let me do that neither.

Without being aware again, I was changed leadership style: my team had promoted me from "supporting" to "delegating".

Silly me, I felt bad because I could not do anything in a project I started doing everything. Even worse, I was no longer in the driver's seat. My project was driven by other, and he didn't even let me go as the copilot!

As you might have guessed, the next morning all tests were passed and documented. It was never easier to close a project. Five months later, the client called me: The other parties were testing against EWRS and had reported some defects. Warranty period had not yet expired, so we had to do defect repair at our cost: Bad luck!

Team members of EWRS project were already working in other projects. I forwarded the client email to Israel. That same afternoon they met, reproduced the case of failure, isolated the problem and developed a fix. I received an email from Israel with the installing instruction to the client. I forwarded his email and so the change management was finished. There was no other issue. The project was still open in our corporate project management information system, but none of them even registered a timesheet hour!

The Project Results

EWRS project finished on time on budget. The first great project result was the product generated. Requirements of performance and quality were achieved. The product was formally accepted by client six months after delivery and subsequent maintenance was minimal.

My bosses came to the idea of producing a commercial product competing in the market of "message brokers". Israel's team was happy to rejoin. After a few weeks they adapted EWRS to a general purpose product, valid to every message interchange. They even invented a brand name and logo —BizLogic, some kind of mixture between the well established in the market competitors BizTalk® and WebLogic®. We nearly got the patent. Unfortunately there was no luck with customers. Maybe the marketing campaign was not good enough.

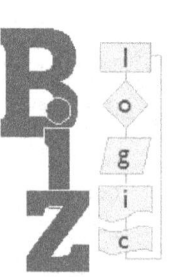

When we presented the project/product in the annual company meeting, we focused very much on these two results: project and product. With the perspective of years, now I think the most relevant result was other: the team. Each team member grew up as an individual thanks to a synergy experience.

As far as I'm concerned, I can say that I really changed from that experience twelve years ago. This was my first time feeling the "magic" that happens when a team forms. When people come together around a common goal, they can exceed all expectations. They add a great value to business. What would have happened if we had been lucky with the customers? They could have set up their own company if they wanted!

I had to live that experience to start thinking these two things: 1) Just to see that team forming magic again forming it is worth doing this and 2) Our goal as Project Managers have to be to get out of detailed work: to delegate.

6.2) I Manage People by Objectives

People assigned to a project should not be managed as if they were workers of an assembly line. Checking how many hours they work, pressing to make them work more unpaid hours, making them feel bad when they leave before us, imposing our criteria offering no explanation, decide for them, showing our rank to make them obey blindly, etc. All this doesn't make them work better. They are knowledge workers. The kind of work they must develop is an intellectual work. Pressing them we don't make them think faster or better. Outstanding team members, those who are the reason of our success, are mainly motivated by personal growth, which is only possible is: 1) their work has meaning for them, that is, short and long term goals are significant to them and 2) they maintain a high level of self control on their work. If we steal a main part of their self control, or if they don't buy the goals, they will understand that their growth possibilities are reduced, and then they don't do voluntarily what we want: They don't follow us yet.

When I started managing projects, I thought my job consisted on controlling all team members did, while their job was to do all as I asked. Since my background was in software programming, my understanding of management was as if work to develop was a system, and people were system modules with interfaces: *Mike and John work together to build that release, that added to Pedro's release by Antonio will be sent to me for review before client acceptance.* To avoid any mistake, I would take each decision and they will wait my instructions. This methodology leads to not much personal and collective development. Back then I had not real synergic and effective teams. The more inefficient was me, unable to delegate. In order to work effectively as a team, I needed to manage by objectives.

The easy part of managing by objectives is monitoring and controlling. The supervised person is supposed to be committed doing as planned. If not, there is a lot of evidence supporting the fact that the goals are not being achieved. You need to be careful here: Kenneth Blanchard[22] warned against negative feedback. Many managers set goals and jut wait to give a reprimand when subordinate makes a mistake. Negative feedback is the first thing they do. This is wrong because they are not growing up on the assignation. It's like teaching a child to walk. If the first time he falls you do a drama, then the child will be afraid and learning will take longer. Conversely, if we say nothing when he falls, but we celebrate when he walks two consecutive steps, then he will learn faster. It is the same with subordinates: you have to wait for their first success and then praise them explaining why that performance is good for us (*in one minute*). These short positive feedbacks reinforce them and make them increase their confidence and control zone. Of course, if they do something wrong you have to give a reprimand[23], but make sure you previously have praised them at least once.

The difficult part of managing by objectives is setting and agreeing on goals. In Covey words, goals should be agreed on: 1) the desirable results; 2) the guidelines on how to do; 3) the available resources; 4) the evaluation mechanisms and 5) the consequences of good and bad performance.

Some other good advice come from Kenneth Blanchard: *Write out each of your goals on a single sheet of paper using less than 250 words (to be read in one minute).*

---

[22] The One Minute Manager, Kenneth Blanchard y Spencer Johnson, Ed. Grijalbo, 2008.

[23] Recall the feedback rule we mentioned in sub-habit 5.1: Don't say "you", say "I".

The main benefit of management by objectives is that people take over. Regarding control, an important point is the method for doing the work. You could believe that it is your responsibility to choose how each task should be performed. But if you force people to use certain methods, then you cannot blame them when they don't achieve the objectives. The excuse, true or not, is that the methods have not worked. It is essential people use their own methods. You may provide guidelines, but you shouldn't oblige.

You have to give them some leeway, some opportunity to choose their own directions and make their own mistakes. Mistakes are important here. If they have control over their choices only to the extent that they make the same ones that you would have made for them, they have no control at all. You will have no right to blame them for not achieving the goals.

Therefore, in order them to do what you want voluntarily you need to manage by objectives, but think of the control paradox: *In order to keep control you have to give it up.* You have to use your authority so sparingly that no one notices that it's being used. You have to create a real sense that control is not completely centralized in your hands, but spread generously over the whole team.

> *The control paradox: In order to keep control you have to give it up*

Like a gifted helmsman, who knows that all use of the rudder increases drag and thus holds the vessel back, you have to steer with the lightest possible touch. Another useful analogy is how a fencer learns to hold his sword as though it were a bird: *too tight and the bird will be injured; too loose and it will fly away.*

6.3) I Value the Differences

It may seem very repetitive a message that has appeared many times throughout this book: Project Managers can only be as effective as their teams are.

> *Project Managers can only be as*
> *effective as their teams*

In sub-habit 1.3) I fight for my people, we mentioned that a Project Manager is really committed when he fights to get the people best fitted. On chapter 3 we mentioned some old inefficient paradigms considering people interchangeable elements[24]. Well, we finally get the sub-habit properly centered on "hiring the best people for the project"[25].

This sub-habit 6.3) I value the differences can be synthesized easily: A team will not be effective unless it is complete and balanced. The knowledge needed to address the tasks could be distributed (*ignorance and knowledge are balanced*), but also, the group have to have the affinity needed to effective collaboration and getting things done.

---

[24] See old paradigms #4: Take a hard line about people goofing off on the job and paradigm #5: The People Store.

[25] This would correspond to the PMBOK® process 9.2 Acquire Project Team.

A Project Manager cannot force the team to be cohesive and synergic, but he can *plant good seeds* looking for people: 1) with good technical skills; 2) collaborative and 3) oriented to results.

If team members are all homogeneous, uniform and equivalent, they are perhaps too good (and they compete too much), or they may be too bad (and nobody notices). Projects in general, especially those more risky, are favored if there is diversity in knowledge, social characters and behavior.

Effective Project Managers usually prefer diversity to uniformity: they prefer balanced teams. A balanced team does not guarantee succeed, but the contrary is more certain: a team will not be effective if not balanced.

> *In order to be effective project teams*
> *have to be complete and balanced*

On the other hand, while the team is forming (which depends much on themselves, not much on the Project Manager), besides providing ideal environmental conditions to work (co-location, team room, equipment, motivation, goal clarification, spare unnecessary problems, etc.), Project Manager should be aware if the team is complete, or some other role is needed.

Much has been written about the different roles that usually appear when people work together and there are many psychological tests used to classify people on those roles.

Some Project Managers have paradigms here: If they know how to classify a person, then they know what can be done to manipulate him, address communication, praise strengths or criticize weaknesses. In my view, these approaches are often not effective when managing projects.

For example, let's imagine someone is a "blue" one according to Relational Awareness Theory[26]. According to this theory, this person will be motivated by protection, growth and welfare of others. If this person is "red", then motivation comes from completing tasks and getting things done. If "green", then he will take care that the methods used are correct. So, when communicating with a "blue" you must talk about what people are going to get and learn. If a "red" you have to talk about plan to action. If "green" you have to talk about methodology to be used. I wish it were that simple!

I think it's good to know the type of our teammates, it helps us to understand their behaviors and motivations better. It is also good to understand ourselves. The key question is whether classifying people it's worth doing in order to deliver projects on time, on budget, with the right scope and quality. Recall that a project is a natural (not artificial) system which follows the law of the harvest. With team members there are no quick recipes. Using Covey words: *With people fast is slow and slow is fast.*

---

[26] Relationship Awareness Theory, by psychologist Elias Hull Porter (1914–1987).

For an Effective Project Manager, is worth knowing if the team is complete and balanced, or there is some gap to fill. That is more likely on their control zone. Using the analogy with "Complete Person" paradigm, the **"Complete Team" paradigm** should cover these four intelligences:

- **Results** (physical intelligence): Result orientation. Discipline and perseverance to get things done.
- **Skills** (mental intelligence): Knowledge orientation. Having the training and skills needed to develop the work.
- **Collaboration** (emotional intelligence): People collaboration orientation. Teamwork understanding and coordination.
- **Transcendence** (spiritual intelligence): Becoming an outstanding asset as team inside the performing organization. Becoming a self-managed team able to repeat success if join again in a similar project.

> *Complete team paradigm: Balance among Skills, Results, Collaboration and Transcendence*

The English psychologist Dr. Raymond Meredith Belbin, on his book *"Management Teams"* [27] concluded experimentally that the members of an effective team should cover 9 roles when managing and executing work:

---

[27] Management Teams, R. Meredith Belbin, Ed. John Wiley & Sons, 1988.

- Roles oriented to **thought**: Plan, Monitor-Evaluator, and Specialist.
- Roles oriented to **action**: Shaper, Implementer, and Finisher.
- Roles oriented to **people**: Coordinator, Team Worker, and Resource Investigator.

Belbin roles[28] match the Complete Team Paradigm:

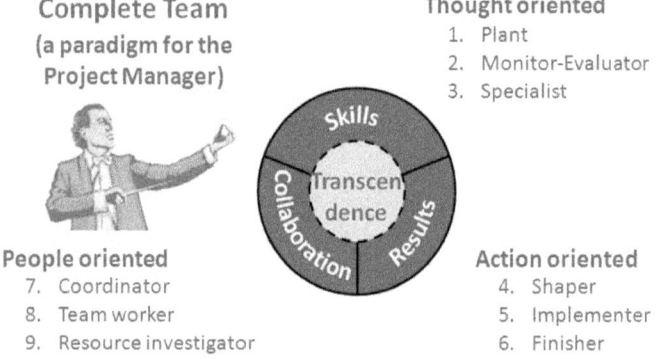

Complete Team
(a paradigm for the
Project Manager)

Thought oriented
1. Plant
2. Monitor-Evaluator
3. Specialist

People oriented
7. Coordinator
8. Team worker
9. Resource investigator

Action oriented
4. Shaper
5. Implementer
6. Finisher

Although Belbin doesn't propose a role oriented to "team transcendence", this classification is useful enough for a Project Manager to analyze if his team is complete and balanced, and then take the best decision on his best judgment.

The table on the following page is a brief description of each of these 9 Belbin's roles, indicating on each role its typical main contribution and weaknesses.

---

[28] You can find a detailed description on Belbin's team roles at: http://goo.gl/ZUp6z

Thought	1. Plant	A creative, imaginative, unorthodox team-member who solves difficult problems. *They sometimes situate themselves far from the other team members, they always come back to present their brilliant idea.*
	2. Monitor-Evaluator	They are best at analyzing and evaluating ideas that other people come up with. They are shrewd and objective and they carefully weigh the pros and cons of all the options. *They are often perceived as detached or unemotional; poor motivators; react to events rather than instigating them.*
	3. Specialist	They have specialized knowledge that is needed to get the job done. They commit themselves fully to their field of expertise. *They focus on technicalities at the expense of the bigger picture.*
Action	4. Shaper	A dynamic team-member who loves a challenge and thrives on pressure and possesses the drive and courage required to overcome obstacles. *They may be seen argumentative, and offend people's feelings.*
	5. Implementer	Practical thinkers, they get things done. They are typically conservative, disciplined people who work systematically and efficiently and are very well organized. *On the downside, they may be inflexible and can be somewhat resistant to change.*
	6. Finisher	They have a great eye for spotting flaws and gaps and for knowing exactly where the team is in relation to its schedule. Emphasizes the need for meeting schedules, deadlines, and completing tasks; searches out errors. *They may worry unnecessarily, and may find it hard to delegate.*
People	7. Coordinator	Mature, confident, identifies talent. Clarifies goals. They are calm and good-natured and delegate tasks very effectively. *They may delegate away too much personal responsibility, and may tend to be manipulative.*
	8. Team worker	They fill the role of negotiators: They are flexible, diplomatic, and perceptive. *They tend to be indecisive, and to maintain uncommitted positions during discussions and decision-making.*
	9. Resource Investigator	Outgoing, enthusiastic, communicative. Looking for new opportunities. They develop contacts. *They may lose enthusiasm quickly, and are often overly optimistic.*

Table 1: Belbin's Team Roles

4. The Habits of Effective Project Managers

4.7 Habit 7. Performing Better the Next Project

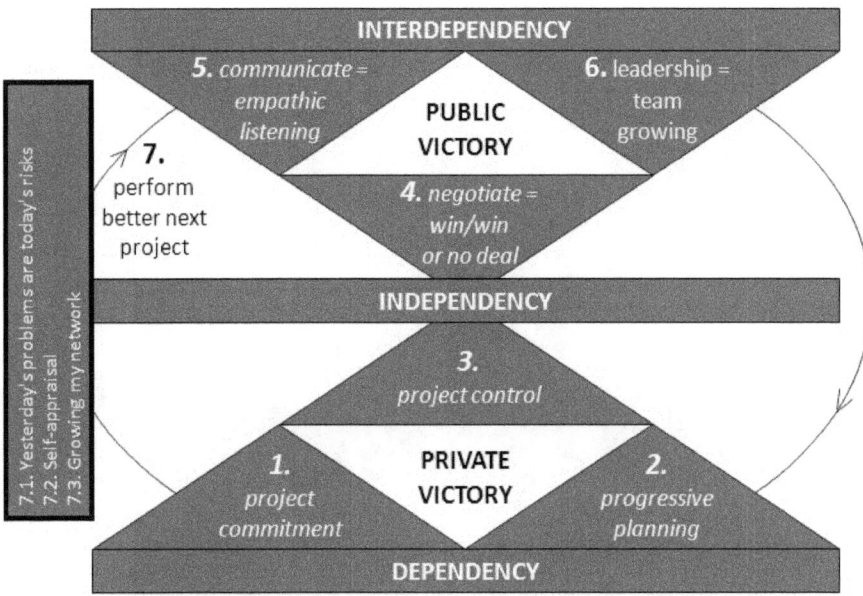

It isn't what you don't know that gets you into trouble.
It's what you know for sure that just isn't so.

MARK TWAIN

4. The Habits of Effective Project Managers

The 7th Habit of Effective People: Sharpen the Saw

The seventh habit of highly effective people, according to Covey is "sharpen the saw". Effective people devote time not only to "cutting the tree" (production: getting the golden eggs) but also to "sharpening the saw" (production capacity: feeding the goose). The principle of renovation, or continuous improvement, is important to be effective: we have to fight sedentary habits, the experience is more and more complex, public victories are more and more interdependent, and our scheme of values has to be constantly reinforced.

The time we devote to self-renewal belongs to the category of important but not urgent (quadrant II, the quadrant of effectiveness). There are many other tasks important but not urgent (*big rocks*) we need to solve week after week to get a feeling of fulfillment and personal effectiveness.

Continuous improvement, in order to be complete, has to include the four intelligences of the complete person paradigm:

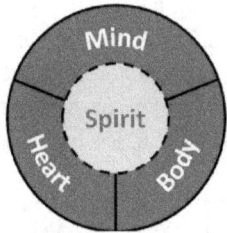

- ▪ **Body**: Exercise, good nutrition, stress control.
- ▪ **Mind**: Reading, visualizing, planning, writing.
- ▪ **Heart**: Service to others, empathy, synergy.
- ▪ **Spirit**: Value clarification, commitment, study, meditation.

The 7th Habit of Effective Project Managers: Perform Better the Next Project

Effective Project Managers should have "their 4 intelligences well sharpened" as effective people. Regarding their job, they need to know that in this profession you never stop learning, and you learn by practice. This is a continuous learning process, each project a new challenge, and the true lessons the mistakes made.

> *Project management is learned by practice: This is a continuous learning process, each project a new challenge, and the true lessons the mistakes made*

After managing a few projects, you realize that on project N you are more prepared than in project N-1. Not a bit more prepared, but *much more* prepared. If the project has been a challenging one (and we have lived it as complete persons) maybe the 6 months of duration are worth 2 years of professional development. You cannot compare two project managers on the basis of years of experience (Project Manager's performance appraisals are still a hard topic for most Human Resource Departments).

Since our first projects we are aware of we don't know everything. We know we need to ask to other Project Managers, to research on tools, to network with colleagues, to attend PMI® meetings, etc.

Effective Project Managers are used to reexamining constantly: 1) what went wrong in the project; 2) what he could improve by himself and 3) how can he make his professional network grow.

7.1) Yesterday's Problems are Today's Risks

Imagine you are starting a new project and somebody tells you: This project is very similar to that just concluded by Peter, why don't not you ask him? You are busy preparing the kickoff meeting. You think this project has been poorly sold and will take longer. You are discovering there are many stakeholders opposing the project, scope is not well delimited, there is much innovation and much to lose if the project goes wrong. You decide to refresh a bit and go to see Peter, a very methodological colleague who has compiled a risk repository structured in cards like these:

There you are the problems that Peter imagined that could happen, the response he planned and after materialization, he annotated final cost overrun and delay. You were beginning to imagine some of these problems on your blank sheet. How much would you pay for something like that?

Leon Tolstoi wrote: "Happy families are all alike; every unhappy family is unhappy in its own way". Likewise, we could say that happy projects are all alike, but the drama we live in every failed project is so particular. You know you are not going to suffer exactly the same problems as Peter, but if we have to use the crystal ball, you better reuse Peter's experience. Okay, Peter's client company was more mature, you are not going to have so many final users and change management will be simpler. Your project and Peter's are different. Still, there are patterns, categories, processes, templates, etc. more or less reusable with low effort —*all a Project Manager may need is already invented.*

In projects, mistakes are paid. Nobody will return you a lost day at the beginning of the project —i.e. you assumed your team would have an equipped room, but you didn't. You get a great benefit just for not stumbling over the same stone twice.

> *Projects mistakes are paid. Effective Project Managers tries not to "stumble over the same stone twice"*

If we don't have *the right to believe* that a particular assumption is still valid, it is our responsibility not to believe. Recall the quote by Mark Twain: "It isn't what you don't know that gets you into trouble. It's what you know for sure that just isn't so."

One of the best habits an Effective Project Manager might have is to collect progressively (involving the rest of stakeholders) the information on risks and lessons learned. Real learning comes only when they write all this down, not just for them, but for others can use this knowledge in the future.

7.2) Self-Appraisal

Effective Project Managers have a personal commitment with continuous improvement: Better to brag about the achievements of the project, they prefer to analyze what has gone wrong and why. They have the habit of identifying their constraints thanks to stakeholders' feedback they continually ask. They want to improve on each project to "perform better the next project".

Effective Project Managers have the habit to talk to other Project Managers (internal mentors or external coaches) on the problems they are suffering on their projects, the processes and tools they are using, lessons learned, improvement areas, etc. This also strengthens their professional network.

7.3) Growing my Network

Success for Effective Project Managers (as consistently delivering on time, on cost, on scope, meeting the quality standards) is proportional to the strength of their relationships. When they don't know how to approach an activity, *they know the phone of the person who knows*. In this Information Society interdependent world, where we only have partial information for everything, it's essential to be well connected.

Fortunately, Project Managers have many ways of socialization. You have professional networks within and out of your company. You have formal and informal networks. To grow your professional network, it's effective to attend monthly local PMI® Chapter meetings, for instance, and belong to social networks at LinkedIn, Twitter, Facebook, etc. Thanks to the Internet, distance is not a barrier anymore.

4. The Habits of Effective Project Managers

5

Maturing as an Effective Project Manager

We must not cease from exploration
And the end of all our exploring
will be to arrive where we began
and to know the place for the first time

T.S. ELIOT

5. Maturing as an Effective Project Manager

Stephen Covey said there is a sequential maturity path to be effective as people. Analogously, we can say there is a sequential maturity path to be an Effective Project Manager. This *continuum* of maturity path for effective people (dependency-independency-interdependency) serves us to recognize the three maturity stages to get an Effective Project Manager.

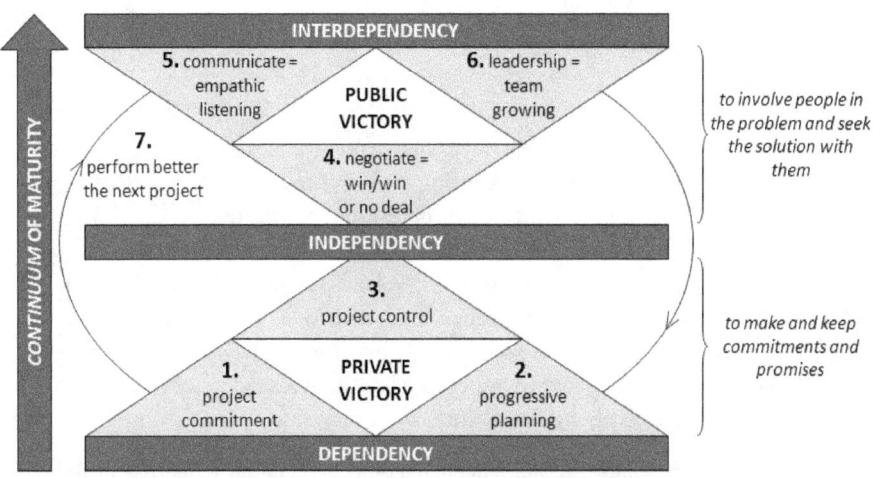

If a person depends on others (physically, emotionally or intellectually) he or she will not have the needed self confidence to make and keep commitments and promises. When we are independent, we are used to getting private victories and reinforce our self confidence and self esteem, but we are not effective really. In this knowledge society everything is interconnected. What we do in isolation is not usually very relevant. Being independent, we are ready to teamwork. With good habits we can get from independency to interdependency. This is a sequential inside-out approach: Private Victories precede Public Victories.

- **Dependence** is the paradigm of "YOU": *You take care of me. You come through for me. You didn't come through. I blame you for the results.*
- **Independence** is the paradigm of "I": *I can do it. I am responsible. I am self-reliant. I can choose.*
- **Interdependence** is the paradigm of "WE": *We can do it. We can cooperate. We can combine our talents and abilities and create something greater together.*

Sequential inside-out approach says that making and keeping promises to ourselves precedes making and keeping promises to others. It is futile to try to improve relationships with others before improving ourselves. But this continuum of maturity is not just an *arrow*. It is more an *upward spiral of growth*. The habit of sharpening the saw leads us to progressively higher forms of responsible independence and effective interdependence. As Covey said: "Sharpening the saw is the habit of renewal: It lifts you to new levels of understanding and living each of the habits as you come around to them on a progressively higher plane."

With good habits, any Project Manager could become an Effective Project Manager, but you could not find any book explaining any linear to get there. Since projects are natural not artificial systems, nobody can guarantee a sustainable success. Effective Project Managers have this in common: They are people of good character. Their character is forged with good habits. Their habits are based on principles. Let's recall the main subject of this book: Good habits make Success in Project Management.

> *Good habits make Success in Project Management*

As we will see in appendix I. Performance appraisal for Project Managers, PMI® already provides a standard on competencies for Project Managers. However, this standard is not practically applicable overall. Could we assess Project Managers' performance by assessing their habits?

Accept the Role, know how to play, and play good

Do you remember the questions and answers about the rules of the game of Project Management in chapter 2? Now we find the habits behind each answer.

–Question #1: They put me in charge of a critical project. They have appointed the team members. They have set the goals, the budget, the schedule; but they have also made me accountable of the whole thing. Is this good or bad?

–Answer: This is something good for you. This means the company you are working for trusts you. You have a challenge ahead, much to learn and demonstrate. This has to do with habit 1) Committing to the Project.

–Question #2: I'm stumbling brick walls again and again. What do I do?

–Answer: The brick walls are not there to keep us out; the brick walls are there to give us a chance to show how badly we want something. Again the habit of committing: Habit 1.

–Question #3: Most things lay beyond my control zone. What should I do?

–Answer: The ends justify the means many times. This is the habit of getting things done: Habit 3.

–Question #4: After analyzing what the client has been promised, I think it is impossible to meet the goals.

–Answer: Elaborate a feasible plan. Propose sensible alternatives. Involve the stakeholders in the problem. This is the habit of Progressive Planning: **Habit 2**.

–Question #5: There are many things of this project that I don't know yet. It seems impossible to me to estimate durations, costs, resources, etc.

–Answer: Perform progressive planning elaboration. For the purpose of estimating, take assumptions and check they are still valid. Keep an updated planning as discovering new project information: **Habit 2**.

–Question #6: This project is prone to uncertainty. I keep talking on risks all the time, but everybody seems to ignore them. What should I do not to be blamed when problems materialize?

–Answer: Keep an updated risk register. On each follow-up meeting, assign time to risk management. The habit of Win-Win or No Deal Managing Risks: **Habit 4**.

–Question #7: My boss' boss wants to be noticed of everything, but he doesn't come to any follow-up meeting. One day the client is going to call him to complain, he is not going to know what to respond, and it will be a cascade of reprimands until me. How should I avoid this?

–Answer: Adapt communication to stakeholders. Top managers usually appreciate periodic status summarized reports; dashboards with color health check indicators; milestone schedules, etc. This the habit of effective communication: **Habit 5**.

–Question #8: Client does not know what he wants. What he is demanding is loose and ambiguous. When we deliver the product, he is going to say "No" to everything. What should I do?

–Answer: Practice incremental iterations, delivering once part of the product each time, first the important ones, so that they can validate progressively: Habit 5.

–Question #9: Client wants to introduce changes continuously.

–Answer: You won't allow that. An effective technique to avoid scope creep is an integrated change management system: Habit 3.

–Question #10: Assigned team members do not have much previous experience in something like this project. They have never worked together. It seems that the only real expert is me. Should I have to do most of the work myself?

–Answer: Get your team members get the training they need, and practice a situational leadership, adapting your leadership style to the maturity of your team. The habit of leadership: Habit 6.

Following there is an incomplete description of strengths (and weaknesses) that I have observed on my colleagues (and myself). Of course, these features don't determine effectiveness, nor explain Project success or failure, but they aim to recognize certain patterns on Project Manager's maturity.

Dependent Project Managers

In the first stage of maturity as Project Managers, we have the *Dependent Project Manager*. Let's see some common patterns of their behavior:

Dependent
- Victim. Blaming others
- Avoidance. Procrastination
- "I will do it myself"

- They are always complaining and blaming others (sales manager, client, managers, team, etc.). They don't truly commit to project goals (habit 1). They don't plan remaining work (habit 2). They don't control the project to get things done when they are due (habit 3).

- Since they lack on habit 3) Project Control, they don't cope with urgent issues, so they never have time to communicate, to guide and motivate team; to manage expectations; to measure performance on schedule, cost, customer satisfaction, etc. When they are asked something, they tend to avoid with the excuse they have many urgent issues to attend. If they have to do something important today what they don't like, they self justify to do it tomorrow.

- Since they lack on habit 6) Team Growing, they are not used to delegating. They take all decisions. They often do some technical work. We hear them say: "It takes less doing than explaining."

Do you remember the list of flaws we recollected in chapter 1? Following there are some of the flaws that could be attributed to a *Dependent Project Manager* (the list is not complete):

- *He is always complaining about the organizational processes, the lack of resources, the customer, the deadlines, etc., but he never proposes any solution* (he scores low on <u>habit 1</u>).
- *He is not a proactive person. He does not anticipate problems. He proceeds reactively, crisis after crisis* (<u>habit 1</u>).
- *He takes too long to make any decision. I don't see him having clear criteria regarding the project* (<u>habit 2</u>).
- *He has not prepared any formal or informal project plan. If I ask him, he does that, but I suspect it's just for the record* (<u>habit 2</u>).
- *He does not manage time well. He is always overwhelmed. He never seems to have time for anything new. He does not respond to email. He does not call back. The urgent does not let him do the important. He is not used to keeping his promises* (<u>habit 3</u>).
- *He lacks the drive to close the project. He has the 90% complete syndrome.* (<u>habit 3</u>).
- *He does not maintain a project log. He does not manage scope well.* (<u>habit 3</u>).
- *He is not concerned about the budget, the actual costs, the invoiced cost, the financial margin, etc.* (<u>habit 3</u>).

Independent Project Managers

In the second stage of maturity, the Project Manager has already good self esteem. He is used to "making and keeping commitments and promises". He doesn't blame others systematically. He is capable to commit, plan and control the project. However, when the Project is suffering big problems, or when dramatic changes on expectations are needed, he is not used to "involving people in the problem and seeking the solution with them."

Independent
- We want to be like Rowan
- Halo Effect. Domain Expertise. Hard Skills
- "Can Do" Thinking. Plan for Success

■ An Independent Project Manager wants to be like **Rowan** (recall A Message To Garcia[29]). He is used to getting things done in an environment of uncertainty, acting beyond his circle of influence. The thinks vey often that *the ends justify the means*. This attitude backfires when ignoring the habits necessary to get public victories. He gets short time results but he is not feeding *the goose that produce golden eggs*. Remember that, with people, *slow is fast and fast is slow*.

---

[29] You can read the original text at: http://goo.gl/l9S2g

▪ *Independent Project Managers* usually have a lot of **domain expertise**. They are quite competent in technology and processes applicable to their specific industry. Since they have good domain expertise, they are supposed to lead teams and projects, so they are put in the position of a Project Manager (this is called "**the halo effect**"). They are usually interested in improving their skills on tools, techniques and processes or project management (**hard skills**). Many of them get Project management accreditations. Unfortunately, these capabilities are quite often not enough. *Independent Project Managers* usually are good managing *gantts*, monitoring and controlling activities assigned to team members, keeping documents up to date, etc. Also very often, we see them that burn the team out, reach win-lose agreements with stakeholders, ignore the real requirements, quality criteria, needed changes, etc.

▪ *Independent Project Managers* usually say no to certain changes impacting negatively on schedule (sub-habit 2.3). Conversely, sometimes they persuade themselves to believe certain goals are possible, when they don't have the right to believe so. The big boss calls for extraordinary performance and he says "Yes! We can do it". This is the expected submission and acceptance of challenges. Unfortunately "**Can Do Thinking**" also known as "**Plan for Success**" is antithetical to effective Risk Management (sub-habit 4.3).

Some typical flaws of an *Independent Project Manager*:

- *He says the client yes to everything* (he scores low on habit 2 & habit 4).
- *He does not provide executive reporting. For instance, he is not able to measure the current progress, nor forecast the final slippage and cost overrun* (habit 3 & habit 5).
- *I have so many complaints from the functional managers, from the client, from the sellers, etc. He has not a good rapport with stakeholders: they don't trust him* (habit 4 & habit 5).
- *He is not used to delegating. He has to take every decision himself. He goes too deep on technical details* (habit 6).
- *He is too authoritarian. He has burned the team out* (habit 6).
- *I see him making the same mistakes. He stumbles over the same stone twice. I think he is not concerned about improving* (habit 7).

Interdependent Project Managers

Upward spiral of growth for an Effective Project Manager starts when he is used to "involving people in the problem and seeking the solution with them". On each project, he wants to achieve the product of the project but also the *team* of the project: A real cohesive synergic team capable of facing a subsequent similar project without supervision. He is confident on managing and taking decisions (*he take the technical cap off and put the manager cap on*), but he is also used to get public victories thanks to effective communication, managing expectations and solving problems involving others.

Interdependent
- "Can't Do" Thinking. Plan for Failure
- Soft Skills. Involving Expert Judgment
- Principle-Centered Leadership

An *Interdependent Project Manager* recognizes the importance of managing risks. He checks assumptions constantly. He asks himself "Do we have the right to believe in this budget, this schedule, this expected performance?" If he has only time to manage one area, he devotes to managing risks. He knows that people aren't really bad at estimating. What people are really bad at is enumerating all the assumptions that lie behind estimates. He wants to anticipate anything that could be wrong. He prefers **Planning for Failure** better than Planning for Success. He acknowledges the **Can't Do Thinking** possibilities and approaches what he has not the right to believe as risks to be explicitly managed.

- *Interdependent Project Managers* sow solid relationship among their professional network. They foster continuous improvement thanks to the feedback they get from clients, managers and team. They try to improve mainly two types of soft skills: 1) communication (they are aware that until product delivery, the only thing stakeholders can see is communication) and 2) leadership (so that team can grow). They don't usually take the technical decisions. They prefer to involve **expert judgment**. Their domain expertise is secondary. Their main goal is to coordinate what others do, better than doing themselves (they resembles to orchestra directors).

- Last, but not least, an *Interdependent Project Manager* plays the four roles of **principle centered leadership**: 1) He is a model of integrity and a reference to others; 2) He doesn't impose a way of doing things, but consider advice and recommendations from others; 3) He tries to align work with processes, structure and systems at the corporate level and 4) He delegates work to people, according to their skills.

Appendix

Appendix

I. Performance appraisal for PMs

In 2002, PMI® published the first version of the standard "Project Manager Competency Development (PMCD) Framework". In 2007 PMI® released the second edition. The main goal was to provide a guide to evaluate and manage the professional development of Project Managers.

Organizations should adapt this framework to their own needs. The standard assumes that competent Project Managers must show, by means of evidences, that they are proficient in three areas: Knowledge Skills, Performance Skills and Personal Skills.

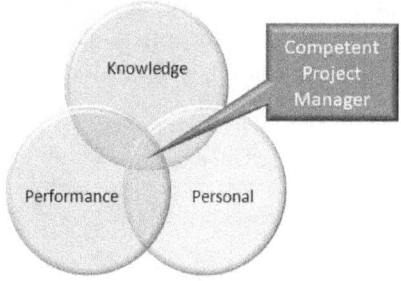

- **Project Management Knowledge**: They have the knowledge to manage project initiating, planning, executing, monitoring and controlling, and closing.
- **Project Management Performance**: The ability to apply project management knowledge to achieve project goals.
- **Personal Competency**: How they behave when managing projects, their attitudes and personal values.

According to PMI®, Project Management Knowledge is represented by the knowledge of the standard PMBOK®. Project Managers demonstrate this knowledge if they get the CAPM® credential (*Certified Associated in Project Management*) or the PMP® credential (*Project Management Professional*). For this reason, the standard is focused on developing performance and personal competences.

Performance competences are developed in 5 competences units, which are broken down into 30 performance elements, which are broken down into 122 performance criteria, which are broken down into 168 types of evidence.

Personal competences are developed in 6 competences units, 25 performance elements, 90 performance criteria, and 251 types of evidence.

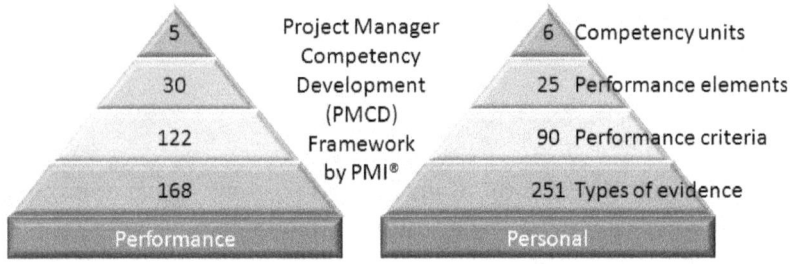

Let's see two examples of performance elements, one from performance competences and the other from personal competences.

Element of performance competence: *1.5 Project Charter Approved.*

1.0. Unit of Competence: Initiating a Project

Performing the work to authorize a new project and define its scope

Element 1.5 Project charter approved

Performance Criteria	Types of Evidence
1.5.1. Develops a high-level project strategy	1.5.1.1. Documented high-level project strategy
1.5.2. Establishes the project's key milestones and deliverables	1.5.2.1. Documented milestones and deliverables
1.5.3. Develops summary budget	1.5.3.1. Documented order of magnitude effort estimate
1.5.4. Supports the project charter preparation	1.5.4.1. Documented resource requirements 1.5.4.2. Document summary budget 1.5.4.3. Draft project charter documents
1.5.5. Uses governance process to obtain sponsor approval and commitment	1.5.5.1. Approved project charter, with governance documentation (e.g. business cases, stage gate meeting minutes)

This performance element is one out of five in the competence unit: *1.0 Initiating a Project.* There are other four competence units: *2.0 Planning a Project; 3.0 Executing a Project; 4.0 Monitoring and Controlling a Project* and *5.0 Closing a Project.*

Element of personal competence: *10.1 Resolves Project Problems.*

10.0 Unit of Competence: Effectiveness	
Produces desired results by using appropriate resources, tools and techniques in all project management activities	
Element 10.1 Resolves project problems	
Performance Criteria	Types of Evidence
10.1.1. Employs appropriate problem solving techniques	10.1.1.1. Documented needs analysis (e.g., design inputs list) 10.1.1.2. Documented feedback from stakeholders of problem solving techniques 10.1.1.3. Documented use of proper knowledge management tools 10.1.1.4. Issue log with resolution documentation
10.1.2. Validates that proposed solutions resolve the problem and are within the project boundaries	10.1.2.1. Documented use of proper knowledge management tools 10.1.2.2. Issue log with resolution documentation 10.1.2.3. Documented feedback from stakeholder the problems were solved
10.1.3. Chooses solutions that maximize project benefit and minimize negative impacts	10.1.3.1. Documented feedback from stakeholder stating the problems were 10.1.3.2. Documented impact of solution on project 10.1.3.3. Documented external and/or environmental impact of solution

This performance element is one out of four in the competence unit: *10.0 Effectiveness*. There are other five competence units: *6.0 Communicating; 7.0 Leading; 8.0 Managing; 9.0 Cognitive Ability* and *11.0 Professionalism*.

Therefore, any performance appraisal system based on PMI® standard should consider more than 400 possible evidences. Appraisers should be able to score more than 200 performance criteria. This extraordinary complexity makes such a system quite impracticable.

On the other hand, it does not seem very "natural" this way of judging Project Managers, so systematically, by means of evidences. If we agree on the statement "a project should only finish when stakeholders meet or exceed their expectations", then the best way to assess performance is a satisfaction survey.

When measuring soft skills, it does not seem quite wise looking for written evidence on how effective a Project Manager has been. Maybe that Project Manager we are evaluating has a real domain expertise and yet he never has heard of the PMBOK®. Going back to those two examples above: We could have someone who initiates the project brilliantly without writing a Project Charter. We could have someone who solves a conflict outstandingly without writing a line (maybe what he did was talking to people involved or simply made them talk).

Performance Appraisal Systems should be kept simple and understandable by everyone. There is no other profession more goal oriented than Project Management. Hence, you can measure Project Managers competence by measuring their project results on every project. You may not have to evaluate theoretical and practical knowledge, since the means are implicit in the ends.

If the project ends up with a 50% of cost overrun, and this is a big surprise, it is clear that Project Manager has not controlled the cost performance baseline, but we don't need to evaluate if he is proficient about tools and techniques. What is the point of assessing if he is proficient or not in Earned Value Management? He has not met the project cost goal, period. If the project ends up with every team member burnt out, it is evident this Project Manager has to improve his soft skills.

The paradigm of 7 habits of effectiveness can be seen as a structure of competences needed by a Project Manager to get private and public victories, to be regularly successful managing projects.

Stephen Covey said that the fairest evaluation system for knowledge workers is a 360° performance appraisal system based on the 7 habits paradigm. The evaluated person, his managers, colleagues and direct reports could easily score each of the 7 habits.

This book recommends this alternative way of evaluating Project Managers, using the 7 habits of an Effective Project Manager.

One example of appraisal result could be as represented bellow:

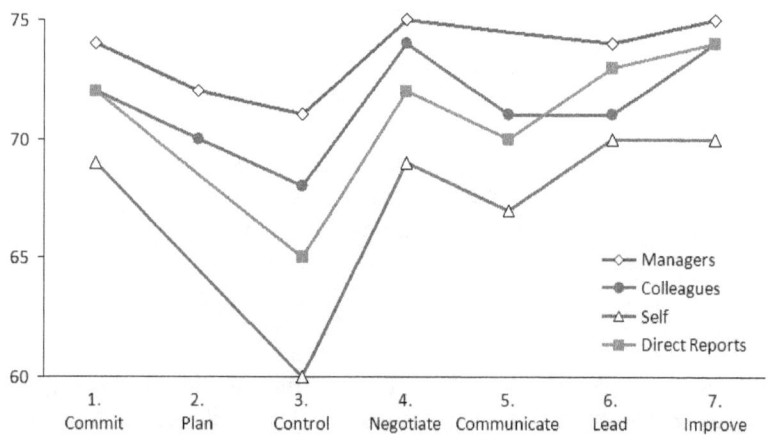

When the project is finished, every stakeholder (client, sponsor, manager, PMO, experts, team members, etc.) will have a valid opinion on the Project Manager performance. Everybody should know how to respond to questions like:

1. Has the Project Manager been truly committed to the project?
2. Has the Project Manager clarified what to do, early enough?
3. Has the Project Manager controlled scope, schedule and cost?
4. Has the Project Manager managed properly uncertainty and conflicts?
5. Has the Project Manager communicated effectively?
6. Has the Project Manager been a good leader?
7. Has the Project Manager learned valuable things?

Appendix

II. Code of Ethics and Professional Conduct by PMI®

This Code[30] applies to all PMI® members; non-members who hold a PMI certification; non-members who apply to commence a PMI certification process and non-members who serve PMI in a volunteer capacity.

Throughout several studies conducted by PMI, practitioners from the global project management community were asked to identify the values that formed the basis of their decision making and guided their actions. The values defined as most important were: **responsibility, respect, fairness**, and **honesty**. This Code is divided into sections that contain standards of conduct which are aligned with the four values. Each section of the Code includes both aspirational standards and mandatory standards[31]:

- The **aspirational standards** describe the conduct that we strive to uphold as practitioners. Although adherence to the aspirational standards is not easily measured, conducting ourselves in accordance with these is an expectation that we have of ourselves as professionals—it is not optional.

- The **mandatory standards** establish firm requirements, and in some cases, limit or prohibit practitioner behavior. Practitioners who do not conduct themselves in accordance with these standards will be subject to disciplinary procedures before PMI's Ethics Review Committee.

---

[30] PMI® document can be downloaded at: http://www.pmi.org

[31] Aspirational standards and mandatory standards are not mutually exclusive; that is, one specific act or omission could violate both aspirational and mandatory standards.

Project Managers should act with RESPONSIBILITY

Responsibility is our duty to take ownership for the decisions we make or fail to make, the actions we take or fail to take, and the consequences that result.

Aspirational Standards:

- We make decisions and take actions based on the best interests of society, public safety, and the environment.
- We accept only those assignments that are consistent with our background, experience, skills, and qualifications[32].
- We fulfill the commitments that we undertake – we do what we say we will do.
- When we make errors or omissions, we take ownership and make corrections promptly. When we discover errors or omissions caused by others, we communicate them to the appropriate body as soon they are discovered. We accept accountability for any issues resulting from our errors or omissions and any resulting consequences.
- We protect proprietary or confidential information that has been entrusted to us.
- We uphold this Code and hold each other accountable to it.

---

[32] Where developmental or stretch assignments are being considered, we ensure that key stakeholders receive timely and complete information regarding the gaps in our qualifications so that they may make informed decisions regarding our suitability for a particular assignment. In the case of a contracting arrangement, we only bid on work that our organization is qualified to perform and we assign only qualified individuals to perform the work.

Mandatory Standards:

- We inform ourselves and uphold the policies, rules, regulations and laws that govern our work, professional, and volunteer activities.
- We report unethical or illegal conduct to appropriate management and, if necessary, to those affected by the conduct[33].
- We bring violations of this Code to the attention of the appropriate body for resolution.
- We only file ethics complaints when they are substantiated by facts[34].
- We pursue disciplinary action against an individual who retaliates against a person raising ethics concerns.

---

[33] These provisions have several implications. Specifically, we do not engage in any illegal behavior, including but not limited to: theft, fraud, corruption, embezzlement, or bribery. Further, we do not take or abuse the property of others, including intellectual property, nor do we engage in slander or libel. In focus groups conducted with practitioners around the globe, these types of illegal behaviors were mentioned as being problematic. As practitioners and representatives of our profession, we do not condone or assist others in engaging in illegal behavior. We report any illegal or unethical conduct. Reporting is not easy and we recognize that it may have negative consequences. Since recent corporate scandals, many organizations have adopted policies to protect employees who reveal the truth about illegal or unethical activities. Some governments have also adopted legislation to protect employees who come forward with the truth.

[34] These provisions have several implications. We cooperate with PMI concerning ethics violations and the collection of related information whether we are a complainant or a respondent. We also abstain from accusing others of ethical misconduct when we do not have all the facts. Further, we pursue disciplinary action against individuals who knowingly make false allegations against others.

Out of the five mandatory standards, the first two have to do with "Regulations and Legal Requirements" and the last three refers to "Ethics Complaints".

According to **RESPONSIBILITY** standards, it is appropriate, for instance:

- Accepting challenging assignations, always noticing stakeholders (and taking training if needed).
- Reporting our manager if someone in our organization violates this Code.
- Taking disciplinary action against a team member who lies.
- If a product of the Project, under certain circumstances, could cause health problems, then it is mandatory to retire the product, even when contingency plan costs less, even when put at risk only a single person.

Conversely, it is not acceptable according to **RESPONSIBILITY** standards, for instance:

- Bidding tenders to win contracts for what our Company is not qualified.
- Taking part in illegal activities.
- Ignoring property rights.

Project Managers should act with RESPECT

Respect is our duty to show a high regard for ourselves, others, and the resources entrusted to us. Resources entrusted to us may include people, money, reputation, the safety of others, and natural or environmental resources.

An environment of respect engenders trust, confidence, and performance excellence by fostering mutual cooperation —an environment where diverse perspectives and views are encouraged and valued.

Aspirational Standards:

- We inform ourselves about the norms and customs of others and avoid engaging in behaviors they might consider disrespectful.
- We listen to others' points of view, seeking to understand them.
- We approach directly those persons with whom we have a conflict or disagreement.
- We conduct ourselves in a professional manner, even when it is not reciprocated[35].

---

[35] An implication of these provisions is that we avoid engaging in gossip and avoid making negative remarks to undermine another person's reputation. We also have a duty under this Code to confront others who engage in these types of behaviors.

Mandatory Standards:

- We negotiate in good faith.
- We do not exercise the power of our expertise or position to influence the decisions or actions of others in order to benefit personally at their expense.
- We do not act in an abusive manner toward others.
- We respect the property rights of others.

According to **RESPECT** standards, it is appropriate, for instance:

- Confronting those who do not show respect.
- Getting informed on other's customs.
- Behaving in a professional manner, even when this is not reciprocal.

Conversely, it is not acceptable according to **RESPECT** standards, for instance:

- Taking advantage of our position.
- Making negative, undermining remarks.
- Using abusive language or actions.
- Acting in bad faith.
- Instilling rumors or gossip.
- Ignoring property rights.
- Paying a fee to a government official to ensure our application will be approved faster (that is considered a bribe).

Project Managers should act with FAIRNESS

Fairness is our duty to make decisions and act impartially and objectively.

Our conduct must be free from competing self interest, prejudice, and favoritism.

Aspirational Standards:

- We demonstrate transparency in our decision-making process.
- We constantly reexamine our impartiality and objectivity, taking corrective action as appropriate[36].
- We provide equal access to information to those who are authorized to have that information.
- We make opportunities equally available to qualified candidates[37].

---

[36] Research with practitioners indicated that the subject of conflicts of interest is one of the most challenging faced by our profession. One of the biggest problems practitioners report is not recognizing when we have conflicted loyalties and recognizing when we are inadvertently placing ourselves or others in a conflict-of-interest situation. We as practitioners must proactively search for potential conflicts and help each other by highlighting each other's potential conflicts of interest and insisting that they be resolved.

[37] An implication of these provisions is, in the case of a contracting arrangement, we provide equal access to information during the bidding process.

Mandatory Standards:

- We proactively and fully disclose any real or potential conflicts of interest to the appropriate stakeholders.

- When we realize that we have a real or potential conflict of interest, we refrain from engaging in the decision-making process or otherwise attempting to influence outcomes, unless or until: we have made full disclosure to the affected stakeholders; we have an approved mitigation plan; and we have obtained the consent of the stakeholders to proceed[38].

- We do not hire or fire, reward or punish, or award or deny contracts based on personal considerations, including but not limited to, favoritism, nepotism, or bribery.

- We do not discriminate against others based on, but not limited to, gender, race, age, religion, disability, nationality, or sexual orientation.

- We apply the rules of the organization (employer, Project Management Institute, or other group) without favoritism or prejudice.

---

[38] A conflict of interest occurs when we are in a position to influence decisions or other outcomes on behalf of one party when such decisions or outcomes could affect one or more other parties with which we have competing loyalties. For example, when we are acting as an employee, we have a duty of loyalty to our employer. When we are acting as a PMI volunteer, we have a duty of loyalty to the Project Management Institute. We must recognize these divergent interests and refrain from influencing decisions when we have a conflict of interest. Further, even if we believe that we can set aside our divided loyalties and make decisions impartially, we treat the appearance of a conflict of interest as a conflict of interest and follow the provisions described in the Code.

According to **FAIRNESS** standards, it is appropriate, for instance:

- Recognizing and disclosing our conflict of interests.
- Acting in an open and transparent way.
- Applying and following organizational rules.
- Granting equal opportunities.
- Accepting the invitation to lunch or dinner (this is normal social behavior).
- Accepting a marketing token from a seller.

Conversely, it is not acceptable according to **FAIRNESS** standards, for instance:

- Ignoring our potential conflict of interests.
- Providing more information to a seller than the rest.
- Discriminating.
- Giving favorite trait to relatives to get positions or prizes regardless of merit (nepotism).
- Accepting bribes.
- Expensive gifts are potential conflicts of interest. Companies use to have a policy on this respect (e.g. "a gift can be accepted if it costs less than 100 €"). If there are doubts about whether the gift should be accepted or not, it is recommended to ask a superior.

Project Managers should act with HONESTY

Honesty is our duty to understand the truth and act in a truthful manner both in our communications and in our conduct.

Aspirational Standards:

- We earnestly seek to understand the truth.
- We are truthful in our communications and in our conduct.
- We provide accurate information in a timely manner[39].
- We make commitments and promises, implied or explicit, in good faith.
- We strive to create an environment in which others feel safe to tell the truth.

Mandatory Standards:

- We do not engage in or condone behavior that is designed to deceive others, including but not limited to, making misleading or false statements, stating half-truths, providing information out of context or withholding information that, if known, would render our statements as misleading or incomplete.

---

[39] An implication of these provisions is that we take appropriate steps to ensure that the information we are basing our decisions upon or providing to others is accurate, reliable, and timely. This includes having the courage to share bad news even when it may be poorly received. Also, when outcomes are negative, we avoid burying information or shifting blame to others. When outcomes are positive, we avoid taking credit for the achievements of others. These provisions reinforce our commitment to be both honest and responsible.

- We do not engage in dishonest behavior with the intention of personal gain or at the expense of another[40].

According to **HONESTY** standards, it is appropriate, for instance:

- Providing accurate, complete and reliable information to support decision making.
- Accepting blame.
- Protecting confidentiality of information entrusted to us.
- Providing truthful and accurate information in status reports and press releases.
- If you take over a project and discover that project status information has not been correctly communicated, you should notify them and provide the correct information.

Conversely, it is not acceptable according to **HONESTY** standards, for instance:

- Misleading stakeholders.
- Conceal bad news.
- Taking credit of other's work.
- Burying information.
- Lying or telling half-truths.
- Getting access to confidential information without authorization.

---

[40] The aspirational standards exhort us to be truthful. Half-truths and non-disclosures intended to mislead stakeholders are as unprofessional as affirmatively making misrepresentations. We develop credibility by providing complete and accurate information.

Appendix

III. The Denver Airport Case Study

The following text is based on the book: *Waltzing with Bears: Managing Risk on Software Projects. Ed: Dorset House Publishing, 2003. Tom DeMarco & Timothy Lister.*

The city of Denver, Colorado, set out in 1988 to build a new airport to replace the existing one, Stapleton Airport. Costs would be reduced, pollution and air-traffic delays would be eliminated, and growth would be assured. The new Denver International Airport (DIA) was scheduled to open on October 31, 1993. Finally it was partial opened in 1995, after 500 million dollars of cost overrun. What happened?

On the due date, every other part of the vast airport complex was ready to go. But the software wasn't ready, so the airport couldn't open. Specifically, what wasn't ready on time was the Automated Baggage Handling System (ABHS). An article in Scientific American put responsibility for the DIA disappointment squarely on the software industry and its lax standards and practices. This was a process problem: The delays at DIA might very well have been avoided if only the project had improved its process to include higher CMM level. But an improved software process wouldn't eliminate uncertainty from projects. A deeper analysis would have discovered other reasons.

Let's imagine the following fictional interrogation to the project management team:

–Question: Why couldn't the airport open without the baggage-handling software?

–Answer: The baggage-handling software was on the overall project's critical path for the airport's opening. Passengers couldn't be moved through the airport, even for a single day, without that system.

–Question: Why was the ABHS on the critical path?

–Answer: There was no other way to move the baggage. The system of tele-carts and bar-code readers and scanning devices and switch points and cart unloaders was the only way to get baggage to and from the planes.

–Question: Are there no alternative ways to move baggage?

–Answer: There is, for example, the time-honored method of having big burly guys haul the stuff. There is also the conventional airport approach of small trucks pulling hand-loaded carts, daisy-chained together.

–Question: When the ABHS wasn't ready on time, why couldn't DIA open with one of these alternative methods of moving baggage?

–Answer: The tunnels that were meant to serve the automated tele-cart system were too low for people and couldn't accommodate the trucks.

–Question: Couldn't the tunnels have been redesigned so that trucks and hauled carts could go through them?

–Answer: Yes, but there wasn't time. By the time it was discovered that the ABHS software would be late, the tunnels were already built. And the time to revamp them was judged to be longer than the time required perfecting the software.

–Question: Couldn't the revamping of the tunnels have started earlier?

–Answer: Yes, but that wasn't judged appropriate. Money and time spent on the tunnels would have been wasted had the software actually been delivered on time, as upper management was then assuring it would be.

–Question: Wasn't lateness of the ABHS software seen as a potential risk?

–Answer: Only after it happened. Before that, the software was placed on an aggressive schedule and manager for success.

–Question: Haven't software projects been late before?

–Answer: Yes, but this one was supposed to be different.

–Question: Was there any history of prior projects building similar systems?

–Answer: The Franz Josef Strauss Airport in Munich had installed a pilot ABHS, designed along the lines of the DIA version.

–Question: Did the DIA team visit the Munich project, and if so, what did it learn?

–Answer: Members of DIA's ABHS project did visit Munich. The Munich software team had allowed a full two years for testing and six months of 24-hour operation to tune the system before cut-over. They told the DIA folk to allow that much or more.

–Question: Did DIA management follow this advice?

–Answer: Since there wasn't time for such extensive testing and tuning, they elected not to.

–Question: Did the project team give sufficient warning of impending lateness?

–Answer: When the DIA board of governors first put the ABHS out to bid, nobody was willing to submit a bid for the scheduled delivery date. Eventually, the airport engaged BAE Automated Systems to take on the project on a best-effort basis. During the project, the contractor asserted early and often than the delivery date was in jeopardy and that the project was slipping further behind with each month and each newly introduced change. All parties were made aware that they were trying to do a four-year project in two years. All of this evidence was ignored.

Conclusion: This was a failure of risk management far more than of software process:

- Even the most perfunctory risk management effort would have listed a delay in the software delivery as a significant risk.
- An exposure analysis of this risk would have shown that since the baggage-handling software was on the critical path, any delay would postpone the airport's opening, resulting in financial penalties of $33 million per month.
- From there, it would have been an obvious conclusion that moving the software off the critical path was a key mitigation strategy. A few million dollars spent early in the effort to make an alternative baggage-handling scheme feasible would have saved half a billion dollars from taxpayers.

Who blew it? Don't blame the contractor. Responsibility for risk management accrues to whichever party will have to pay the price for risks that are ignored. In this case, all such costs were eventually paid for by the contracting agency, Denver Airport System.

> *Responsibility for Risk Management accrues to whichever party will have to Pay the Price for Risks that are Ignored*

Effective Project Managers don't want to be blamed for ignoring risks. If risks are ignored in their project they manage expiation by making crystal clear they are not the ones ignoring those risks.

I wonder sometimes: How would end up that Project Manager from BAE Automated Systems?

It is easy to imagine not very good. He surely would bear much of the blame. I hope, at least, he kept an updated risk register explaining specifically the details of one risk: the late delivery of ABHS software. I would be happy if I could find this information about it:

- Risk impact valued as of $33 million per month.
- Recommended risk response: Mitigate by redesigning the tunnels.
- And the most important: The project management team member who decided to passively accept that risk, thinking that he had *the right to believe* that risk was not going to happen. That is: who decided best response was *crossing fingers*.